Snyder

The Holy Card Book
of
Patron and Name Saints

Text
Sheila May McCallum
Anna May McCallum

Artist
Anna May McCallum

ISBN: 0-9761137-0-8

Published, printed and bound in the U.S.A.

Ammccallum, Inc.
10930 243rd Street
Scandia, MN 55073

www.ammccallum.com
ammccallum@usfamily.net

Dedication

This book is dedicated to St. Anne,
my name saint, and to my mother Ann
who is up there with her.

And Father Joseph Frisch
who died before he could do the writings
for this book.
I've been asking for his prayers to help me write.
Thank you, dear ones in the care of the Lord!

Table of Contents

Table of Contents
(Cont.)

"What's in a name?"

What's in a name? is the question asked by Shakespeare in his play *Romeo and Juliet*. The answer according to our Judaic-Christian tradition would be that quite a bit is in a name.

In the scriptures we see that God often intervenes in human affairs to get the right name on a person. Names were often given, or even changed, to indicate something about the person or the task to which a person was called. Almost countless examples of that concern about getting the right name on a person could be given. Perhaps the most interesting example of the concern over getting the right name on a person is that of the naming of John the Baptist. John's father, Zecheriah, was unable to speak until he wrote on a tablet regarding his new son: "his name is John." With that, Zecheriah could again speak. The name John means "God is good," and that surely could be the heading written over the ministry of John and the ministry of Jesus.

In our Christian tradition there has usually been a concern about getting a right name for a person. Popes take new names. Those joining Religious Communities take new names. The giving of a name to a child is related to baptism, and that name is often called the baptismal name. At the present time Church law states that "parents, sponsors, and the pastor are to see that a name foreign to a Christian mentality is not given" (Canon 855). The Catechism of the Catholic Church tells us that the name given in baptism should be that of a Saint, or express a Christian mystery or Christian virtue (#2156).

Today's parents should be concerned that they give a right name - a Christian name - to a child. In naming an infant, people are giving a name to a person who came from the hand of God and is to return to God, and who will carry that name throughout life.

There is an old axiom that holds that a name is an omen. That axiom can indicate to us that a good name given to a person can help to shape the life of that person in ways of goodness and faith and holiness.

The Book of Revelation tells us that the victor will receive "a white stone upon which is inscribed a new name...." (Rev, 2:17). May this book that you hold in your hands help to fashion "new names" for a "new people" in the footsteps of Him who came to make all things new.

Rev. Nicholas Matthew Zimmer
Pastor, St. Peter and Paul's Church
Braham, Minnesota

Baptism

Is the first of the seven Sacraments - "the basis of the whole Christian life, the gateway to life in the Spirit and the door which gives access to the other sacraments."[4.C.F.] Through Baptism we are freed from all sin and its consequences --- totally purified! Yet our frailty from sin remains, such as suffering, illness, death, weakness of character, and concupiscence, the inclination to sin. Yet, this concupiscence "is left for us to wrestle with, it cannot harm those who do not consent but manfully resist by the grace of Jesus Christ."[66] "Indeed an athlete is not crowned unless he competes according to the rules."[67]

To baptize (Gk., baptizein) means to immerse or plunge into water. This symbolizes the catechumen's burial into Christ's death and rising again with Him as a "new creature."[6]

In receiving the name of one or more saints at Baptism, the baptized receive special protection from their intercession with God. Knowing your name saint or saints can start an intimate lifetime relationship with him or her or them and enrich your life. There are many stories of their intervention in our lives.

There will be several more saints' books in color plus holy cards and other items about so many interesting "friends" united to us in the Body of Christ - the Church Triumphant. They are rooting for us. The Church Suffering will also be a holy card and they too are rooting for us in return for our remembrance of them before God.

How grand is our God to unite us so! And how fortunate for us if we set out to know them and make "friends in higher places."

4.C.F.	Council of Florence DS 1314 (Catech of the Cath Church)
66	Council of Trent (1546) DS 1515
67	2 Timothy 2:5
6	2 Cor 5:17 Gal 6:15 c.f. Rom 6:3-4 Col 2:12

St. Adelaide

Widow
December 16
means "of noble birth"

Adelaide's husband, King Lothair of Italy, died only three years after their marriage. Berengarius who usurped King Lothair's throne, treated her with indignity and imprisoned her. There is a cute little legend that tells of Adelaide's escape from prison only to get stuck in a mud puddle becoming totally soiled. At this low moment the German king Otto the Great passing through on horseback stops to help her out, and she in utmost chagrin reaches for her husband-to-be's hand not yet aware of her future blessings in him. Otto married her on Christmas Day and eventually became the Holy Roman Emperor. She bore him five children. Upon Otto's death, her stepson, the new king, estranged Adelaide on account of his wife's influence. Years later in 991, when the widowed daughter-in-law died, the former Empress Adelaide returned to be regent for her grandson. This task was now beyond her strength, although she had the assistance of St. Willigis of Mainz. In her spiritual life she humbly listened to the wise guidance of St. Adalbert of Magdeburg, St. Majolus, and St. Odilo of Cluny. St. Odilo said that she was "a marvel of beauty and grace." She founded and restored monasteries and did much towards the conversion of the Slavs on the empire's eastern border until her death on December 16, 999. Adelaide was canonized around the year 1097.

St. Adelaide, let my good action not be stopped by the obstacles in life. Like you, may I patiently persevere in doing good when I meet up with opposition. Amen.

Adeline, Della, Alice, Aline, Elsie

St. Agatha
Virgin and Martyr
February 5
means "good, kind"

According to legend, Agatha was nobly born in Sicily and martyred in 251. She resisted the governor's advances for their co-habitation so he became suspicious and arrested her for being a Christian. Her flesh was ripped with iron hooks and her breasts cut off. When she still resisted, she was thrown on burning coals and a violent earthquake shook the town. She was quickly taken back to prison where some say she was comforted and healed by St. Peter and again tortured the next day. The terrible torture was too much for her and she died soon after. St. Lucy's mother was healed of hemorrhage at Agatha's tomb, where Agatha, in glory, appeared to Lucy to announce that Lucy herself would soon be a martyr also. They are mentioned together in the Canon of the Mass.

Her martyrdom and early cult are historically certain. The epistle of her Mass speaks of God choosing the weak of the world to confound the wise and strong. More than once her veil has stopped the flow of boiling lava from Mt. Etna when it threatened the town. In His way, God has glorified this pure soul's resistance to the assault of passion. Agatha is the patron of nurses. For centuries her intercession has been invoked by Christians for protection against fires, earthquakes, and breast diseases, especially cancer. Whether because warning of a fire is given with a bell or the molten metal for casting a bell resembles lava flowing, Agatha is also patroness of bell-making.

Let us all rejoice in the Lord celebrating a festival in honor of Blessed Agatha, virgin and martyr, at whose passion the angels rejoice, and give praise to the Son of God.
~Introit of her Mass

Agathe, Ag, Aggie

St. Albert the Great

Bishop and Doctor of the Church
November 15
means "nobly bright, illustrious"

St. Albert was born into a Swabian family living in Bollstadt on the River Danube in 1206. Little is known of his life before he studied at the University of Padua. Albert entered the Dominicans in 1222. His father was angry when Albert left to become a priest, obliging Albert to move to another monastery so his father would not find him and force him to return home. In Cologne, Germany, he began his life-long reputation as an outstanding scholar. When St. Albert was sent to work in Paris he met his brightest student: the young Dominican friar, St. Thomas Aquinas.

St. Albert was an authority in physics, geography, astronomy, mineralogy, alchemy (chemistry), and biology. He initiated scholasticism by applying Aristotle's philosophy to theology. His pupil, St. Thomas furthered this achievement.

St. Albert was the pope's personal theologian and canonist for a brief time. In 1260, he was ordained the Bishop of Regensburg and died peacefully at Cologne on November 15, 1280. He is the patron saint of scientists, medical technicians and technologists.

Quotes of St. Albert:
"If then we possess charity, we possess God, for God is Charity." (1 John 4:8)
"The greater, the more persistent your confidence in God, the more abundantly you will receive all that you ask."

Holy Spirit, font of true wisdom, may the intellectual pursuits of all scientists be for Your greater glory and for the salvation of souls. Amen.

Al, Bert, Albert, Bertie, Alberta, Albertine

St. Alphonsus Liguori
Bishop and Doctor of the Church
August 2

Alphonsus was born of virtuous and distinguished parents near Naples in 1696. At 16 years of age, he was granted doctorates in both civil and canon law. He was very fond of music in the theatre, but removed his glasses so he would not see any evil on stage. He also decided not to marry but continued as a lawyer to please God. During eight years of practice, he was never known to lose a case except his last which made him resolve to finally follow the interior call of a priestly vocation much to the fiery indignation of his father. Throughout the kingdom of Naples he made his mark as a missionary priest of the Oratory. He repudiated pompous oratory and rigor in the confessional.

Alphonsus founded the Redemptorist Order and encountered extreme difficulty and opposition every step of the way. Later he co-founded the Redemptoristines according to a revelation given to Sister Mary Celeste. Besides being a prolific writer and artist, Alphonsus also conducted missions and composed music. He used every moment of his time diligently and though strict, was kind and pure in intention. When he was 66 years old he was ordained a bishop. In 1767, he suffered a life threatening illness that crippled his neck so that he needed a gold straw in his chalice to drink the Precious Blood. For twenty years he suffered from crippling arthritis. In attempting to get royal sanction for the Redemptorists, he was cruelly betrayed and even excluded from the order he had founded, and humiliated by some Church authorities. Eighteen months of these trials were succeeded by ecstasies, prophecy, and miracles. Alphonsus peacefully died just before his ninety-first birthday in 1789. In 1871 he was proclaimed a Doctor of the Church. He is the patron for arthritis sufferers.

Quotes of St. Alphonsus Liguori:
"Nothing but self-will can separate us from God."
"Let us be careful not to repeat to anyone the evil that has been said of him by another. For Scripture warns that he who sows discord is hated by God."

Dear St. Alphonsus, from a brilliant beginning in life, you chose to follow Christ up to His passion and partake of His chalice. Through the Holy Spirit you became a holy bishop and Doctor of the Church. Teach us to love the Will of God as you did. Amen.

Al, Alphonse, Fonzie, Alphonzine

St. Andrew

Apostle and Martyr
November 30
means "strong, manly"

Andrew seems obscured by the dominance of St. Peter, but what a saint! Older brother Andrew led Peter to Jesus after he heard John the Baptist proclaim, "Behold the Lamb of God; behold him who takes away the sins of the world." Andrew and Peter immediately left their fishing nets to follow Jesus. Andrew is the one who points out the boy with the loaves and fishes to feed the multitude. "But what is that among so many?" he asks. After receiving the gifts of the Holy Spirit at Pentecost, he spent his remaining life spreading the Good News until his martyrdom in Achaia. Although it is uncertain, tradition holds that he was crucified, and perhaps even upside down as his brother Peter. Since the 14th century, the X shaped cross has been his symbol. Some of his relics are kept in Amalfi, Italy.

St. Andrew is the patron of Scotland and Russia, fishermen, single women, and those who suffer from gout.

St. Andrew Bobola is among the great Jesuit saints. A zealous preacher and passionate priest, he distinguished himself by his devotion to the sick and dying during an epidemic. He also served as a missionary in Poland where he suffered the constant petty persecutions of anti-Catholics. The Cossacks seized him near Janow. He was tortured with the most revolting barbarity and at last beheaded in 1657. In 1730 his mutilated body was found incorrupt. He was canonized in 1938 by Pope Pius XII and his feast day is celebrated on May 21.

We humbly beseech Thy majesty, O Lord that St. Andrew may unceasingly intercede for us through Our Lord Jesus Christ who lives and reigns forever. Amen.

Andy, Andrea, Andre, Drew

St. Anne

Mother of the Blessed Virgin Mary
July 26
means "full of grace"

From an ancient source attributed to St. James the Apostle, we learn all we know of the Blessed Mother's parents. Joachim and Anne were Mary's parents. Anne was barren and suffered reproach for being childless, as all barren Jewesses did at that time. She mourned this sorrow and God answered her prayers in an extraordinary and unsuspected way; an angel appeared to Anne promising her that she would conceive a child, and she, in turn, promised to give the child to God. In due time, she did conceive, although she was beyond the years of child bearing. Tradition has it that Anne and Joachim kept their promise by presenting their three year old little girl Mary to God in the Temple where the Blessed Virgin Mary was reared and consecrated to God. St. Anne is the patroness of housewives, mothers, cabinetmakers, grandmothers, Canada, Brittany in France, and those suffering from infertility.

Titles from the Litany in Honor of St. Ann:
Offspring of the Royal Race of David
Daughter of the Patriarchs
Faithful Spouse of St. Joachim
Mother of Mary, the Virgin Mother of God
Grandmother of Our Savior
Beloved of Jesus, Mary and Joseph
Example of Piety and Patience in Suffering.

Almighty Father, You answered St. Anne's prayers and rewarded her patient suffering by making her the Mother of the Blessed Virgin Mary and the Grandmother of the Savior. Teach us to be patient and persevering in our suffering, and to hope in Your divine action through these earthly pains. Amen.

Anita, Ann, Anna, Annette, Nancy, Hannah, Nina

St. Audrey or Etheldreda

Abbess, Virgin, Widow

June 23

means "noble counselor"

Of all the Anglo Saxon women saints, Audrey must have been the most popular. Complying with her parents' wishes she married Tonbert and they lived together as virgins until he died three years later. She retired to the Island of Ely, which she inherited from Tonbert, and lived there for a period in secluded prayer. Then she was promised in marriage to Egfrid, who at first agreed to a virginal marriage but later changed his mind. She, being a consecrated virgin, appealed to St. Wilfrid of York. Finally the conflict was settled by the Lord's commanding of the ocean waves which rose high around a hill insolating her from King Egfrid and his troops. Then they understood His Divine Will in regard to Audrey and left her in peace.

Audrey had a double monastery built on Ely and became an austere and holy abbess there until her death. She prophesied that she and a number of her nuns would die from pestilence. When the pestilence struck, she and the exact number she had prophesied died from it. Sixteen years later her body was found incorrupt within her simple wooden coffin and many miracles happened there. She is the patron invoked for neck disease.

A great annual fair called *St. Audrey's Tawdrys* is celebrated in that locale where "tawdrys": cheap necklaces, ribbons, and other trumpery, are sold in her commemoration.

Dear St. Audrey, virginity for some is meant to be temporary until marriage. For others it is a special crown that enhances and strengthens their holiness. Help me to discern what God desires so as to be always pure of heart, either as a consecrated virgin, or otherwise, according to His Will. Amen.

St. Augustine
Doctor of the Church ◆ August 28
means "belonging to the venerable, imperial"

St. Monica
Widow ◆ August 27

Augustine was born in North Africa in 354 to a pagan father named Patricius and St. Monica, a devout Christian. Augustine began walking the wrong path, that of the world and immorality, at the age of sixteen. God had gifted him with an extraordinary intellectual ability. His mother Monica suffered terribly seeing her son fall prey to pagan sects and eventually into Manichaeism. Monica redoubled her prayer and sacrifice when she saw Augustine fall deeper and deeper into the chasm of sin. God heard her prayers, and not only spared her son, but had special plans for him that would mark history. Augustine met St. Ambrose, the Archbishop of Milan, who inspired and sparked his conversion by his sermons. Reading St. Paul's letters, Augustine began to experience the power of the Holy Spirit leading him to follow and serve Christ. Once he converted, he left his former lifestyle and received baptism from St. Ambrose during the Easter Vigil of 387. Augustine then pursued the priesthood. His mother Monica died in November of that year, living long enough to see her son's baptism and determination to be a priest of Christ. Soon after his ordination, the Church recognized his keen intellect, deep piety, and eloquence and made him the Bishop of Hippo, Africa in 395. His two famous books are *Confessions* and the *City of God*. Augustine died in 430. St. Augustine is the patron of theologians and printers. St. Monica is the patron of mothers and married women.

Quotes of St. Augustine:
"The Kingdom of Heaven, O man, requires no other price than yourself. The value of it is yourself. Give yourself for it and you will have it."
"He knows how to live well who knows how to pray well."

Lord Jesus, You created and you love all families. You rejoiced in the triumph of St. Monica's prayers for her son and Your servant St. Augustine. Encourage all parents in their prayers for their children, and through St. Augustine and St. Monica's intercession may Your grace of conversion reach their children's hearts. Amen.

Gus, Augie, Augustina, Gussie, Monique, Mona

St. Barnabas

Apostle and Martyr

June 11

means "man of encouragement"

St. Barnabas, a Jew of the tribe of Levi, was born in Cyprus in the first century. His real name was Joseph, but God inspired the apostles to change it to Barnabas when he sold his farm and laid the money as well as his own time and talents at the service of the apostles and the young Church. The apostles chose Barnabas, "a good man, full of the Holy Spirit and of faith," to oversee the Church in Antioch. His success in Antioch soon forced him to seek an assistant to help him. He enlisted the help of St. Paul and introduced Paul to the other apostles, vouching for his trustworthiness. John Mark (Mark the Evangelist) joined them later. These three left Antioch and set out to evangelize as much of the Roman Empire as possible. After some time, Paul continued his journeys with St. Silas, and Barnabas traveled to Cyprus with John Mark. Little is known of Barnabas beyond this separation. He was stoned to death at Cyprus sometime before 61 AD.

St. Aleydis ◆ June 15

A miraculous revelation happened on the feast of St. Barnabas to a charming and delicate girl of seven named Aleydis, or Alice. Having joined of her own choice the Cistercian community of nuns near Brussels, she quickly became a favorite because of her humility, and charity. Aleydis contracted leprosy soon after she joined the sisters which caused them the greatest sorrow because she had to be isolated from the community. Henceforth, she lived as in the wounds of Christ; her one consolation was Holy Communion. On the feast of St. Barnabas in 1249, Aleydis received the miraculous revelation that she would live one more year. Meanwhile she suffered greatly and even lost her eyesight. Through it all, she offered her suffering up for the souls in Purgatory. At daybreak on the feast of St. Barnabas one year later she happily breathed her last.

Father in Heaven, may I see my obligation to evangelize in the world today, and to enlist others to share in the joyful burden of spreading Your message of love. Grant me the generosity of St. Barnabas who gave all that he possessed to fulfill his mission as an apostle. Amen.

Barney, Barnaby, Aleydia, Alice

St. Bartholomew or Nathaniel

Apostle and Martyr

August 24

Bartholomew means "son of Talmai"

Nathaniel means "gift of God"

Bartholomew, also known as Nathaniel, was one of the twelve apostles chosen by Christ after Jesus spent a night in prayer. He was to be a witness of Jesus' life and teachings. When Philip brought Bartholomew of Cana to meet Our Lord, Jesus praised Bartholomew's honesty and nobility saying, "That is a true Israelite in whom there is no guile."

After Pentecost, Bartholomew evangelized in India, Asia Minor, and finally in Armenia where he was skinned alive and beheaded for Jesus his Master. His relics are kept in a church dedicated to him on a little island on the Tiber River near Rome. He is the patron of plasterers and those who suffer with nervous tics.

Blessed Bartolo Longo, a former Satanist, a devout convert, respected lawyer and champion of the orphaned, lived a long life of 85 years and died on October 15, 1926. His tomb as well as that of his wife is located in the Shrine of Our Lady of the Rosary in Pompeii. He and his wife paid for the education of about 45 seminarians.

The promise of Mary that "one who propagates my Rosary shall be saved" was expressed during the beatification of Bartolo Longo by Pope John Paul II on October 26, 1980.

St. Bartholomea's feast day is July 26. She was a virgin and co-founder of the Sisters of Charity of Lovere.

Dear Father, imprint those qualities of nobility and honesty that St. Bartholomew possessed on Your faithful apostles who endeavor to follow Your designs in their lives. Amen.

Bartley, Barnaby, Bart, Nate, Nathan, Tollie, Bartolo, Bartholomea

Benjamin

Old Testament Patriarch
Fourth Sunday of Advent
means "son of the right hand"

Benjamin was the twelfth and last son of Jacob the patriarch of Israel. Born in Bethlehem, his mother Rachel who died during childbirth called him "son of my sorrow". Jacob renamed the baby "son of the right hand". The next time Benjamin appears in scripture, he is seen accompanying his brothers into Egypt to buy grain from Joseph, their unbeknownst half-brother, who was full brother to Benjamin. He was in charge of distributing grain to peoples stricken by famine from near and far. Joseph recognized his brothers who sold him to the Egyptians years before for twenty pieces of silver. They did not recognize him so Joseph was decided to test their goodness and repentance by hiding his silver drinking cup in Benjamin's grain sack. Accusing Benjamin of stealing it, he made Benjamin a hostage slave. Joseph's older brother Judah then spoke openly and contritely about their past ill-treatment of their lost brother, Joseph. Only then did Joseph reveal that he was their brother and peace was restored in the family.

Benjamin became the patriarch of one of the twelve tribes of Israel. Genesis 49 refers to the wild and warlike nature of the tribe of Benjamin expressing that "Benjamin is a ravenous wolf; devouring prey in the morning, and at evening dividing spoil." Jeremiah the prophet was of the tribe of Benjamin.

There is also a deacon, St. Benjamin, who was imprisoned in Persia and martyred in 421 A.D. after being tormented most cruelly by inserting reeds under his fingernails and the tender parts of his body. Then a knotted stake was inserted into his bowel to rend and tear him. He is invoked for bowel disorders and his feast day is March 31.

O God the Father, we thank You for Benjamin and the holy patriarchs who kept the promise of the Messiah alive until His coming. They were the ancestors of those Israelites who, through the Holy Spirit, made Jesus known to us in the Church. Amen.

Benji, Ben, Bennie, Benny

St. Bernard of Clairveaux

Abbot and Doctor of the Church

August 20

means "bold as a bear"

Bernard was born in 1090 in France. He was blessed by being born into a large and fervent noble family. His six siblings are declared blessed by the Church. His mother is Blessed Alice and his father is Venerable Tescelin. Bernard's personality was witty and attractive, his temperament affable and sweet. After a bit of wavering, Bernard became so convinced of his call to the Benedictine monastery that he persuaded thirty-one men to follow him to Citeaux. Around Easter of 1112, thirty-one men including his four brothers, his uncle, and some friends, led by the twenty-two year old Bernard arrived at the monastery door and requested admittance. Having progressed rapidly, Bernard was sent to found another monastery. Although he was occupied with his order, Bernard was also concerned for the popes of his time, and defended the faith against Abelard's philosophy. It is said that Bernard "carried the twelfth century on his shoulders, and he did not carry it without suffering." Bernard was an eloquent speaker and prolific writer. He composed hymns, poems, and treatises, many of which express his tender and filial love for the Blessed Mother. He died August 20, 1153 surrounded by his spiritual children. St. Bernard is the patron of candle-makers, alpine skiers, and beekeepers.

Quote of St. Bernard:
"The thought that is not rejected produces pleasure, and Pleasure leads to consent; Consent to action; Action to habit; Habit to a kind of necessity; And necessity to eternal death."

Holy Spirit set the youth on fire with love for Your Holy Church. Like St. Bernard, may there be examples among the youth who draw their peers to dedicate themselves to be Your pure temples and Your docile instruments. Amen.

Bernie, Bernal, Barney, Bernadette, Bernarda

St. Blaise

Bishop and Martyr
February 3
means "babbler"

St. Blaise was born in Sebaste in Armenia. According to legends, Blaise, rich and noble, received a Christian education and became bishop while still young. He was a doctor before becoming a priest, and later was ordained bishop of his birthplace. Living during the Christian persecutions in the third century, St. Blaise was in continuous hiding to escape persecution. During the persecutions he lived in a cave in the mountains where only beasts roamed. These he healed of wounds and sickness. They even came just to be blessed. Hunters seeking animals for the amphitheatre found him and took him to Agricolus who ordered him to be scourged and deprived of food. A grateful woman whose pig he healed, provided food and tapers for him in prison. In 316, on the way to his martyrdom he healed a dying boy who was suffocating from a fishbone lodged in his throat. Blaise's flesh was torn by iron combs and then he was beheaded. After his death, devotion to him grew and miracles were attributed to his intercession. It is customary on his feast day that the priest hold two blessed candles at the neck of the faithful, invoking St. Blaise's intercession to prevent throat ailments. St. Blaise is considered the patron of wool combers, wild animals, and those who suffer from throat illnesses. He is one of the original Fourteen Holy Helpers.

O Glorious St. Blaise, who left to the Church a precious witness of faith, obtain for us the gift of preserving and defending that faith which is so wickedly attacked and slandered in these times. Also, obtain for us blessings from afflictions of the throat and intercede for us to use our throats now and forever only for the honor and glory of God. Amen.

St. Brendan

Irish Abbot

May 16

means "sword"

Brendan was a native of County Kerry in Ireland. He was educated by holy saints such as Patrick, Finian, and the great abbess, Ita. Once ordained a priest, he traveled throughout Ireland preaching and eventually evangelized Wales. He returned to Ireland and founded several monasteries. He is called "St. Brendan the Navigator" because it is said that he was the first to sail to America in the sixth century (nine hundred years before Columbus). He died at the age of ninety-four in 578. Brendan was buried in one of the monasteries he founded in Clonfert in County Galway. He is the patron saint of sailors.

There are legends written by the Celtic saints about Brendan. The legend of the sea monsters tells of the feast day Mass of the Apostle St. Paul who sailed many times in the Mediterranean. Brendan and his monks were chanting loudly while celebrating Mass in honor of St. Paul when one of the sailing monks saw a large group of fish below moving faster than their ship. "We shall perish if we sing so loud!" he warned. But Abbot Brendan said, "There is no danger here." And turning he celebrated more solemnly than ever. The monstrous fish rose high on all sides until the liturgy was over, then they went away.

In another legend, white birds began to sing a prayer. The sung prayer consoled the sailing monks who were in the midst of the vast ocean. Inspired, they prayed, "Hear us, O God of our salvation, who art the confidence of all the ends of the earth, and of them that are afar off on the sea."

Almighty God, as You guided St. Brendan's journeys, may the journeys we undertake in Your name be safe and successful in fulfilling Your will. Amen.

Brandon, Brent, Brenda

St. Bruce

Bishop
November 13
from a surname

Bruce was a monk who preferred the life of a worldly, secular priest, immaculately dressed, possessing slaves and horses. Bruce even criticized and belittled his bishop, St. Martin of Tours. Once, a sick man hoping for a cure, asked Bruce for Martin instead. Bruce answered, "If you are in search of that maniac, look over there. As usual he's gazing up into the sky like a lunatic." Martin bore with Bruce patiently. The saint once said, "Since Christ put up with Judas, why shouldn't I put up with Bruce?" Martin prophesied that Bruce would be his successor. Bruce did become the Bishop of Tours, although the people rejected him because of his dubious dealings with women. After much suffering, he reformed his life and his feast day is celebrated only two days after St. Martin's feast day.

"They sat in darkness and gloom, prisoners in want and chains.
Because they rebelled against the words of God and they spurned
The counsel of the Most High.
So He humbled their hearts with troubles, they stumbled and there was no one.
And they cried to the Lord in their distress; and He delivered them from their troubles.
And He brought them out of darkness and gloom. And broke their bonds.
Let them give thanks to the Lord for his mercy, and for His wondrous deeds towards
men,
For He has broken the bronze gates and burst the iron bars." Gratitude for Redemption:
Psalm 106: 10-16

Gracious Father, give to your people a deep gratitude and respect for their pastors so that encouraged by love of the faithful, they will lead their flock towards holiness. Amen.

Bryce, Brice

Charles was born into nobility in Italy in 1538. Young Charles was a true Lombard: energetic, efficient, and full of youthful piety. In 1559, at the age of 21, Charles earned a doctorate in Canon Law. His uncle, Pope Pius IV found Charles apt and worthy of being named a cardinal at the age of 22. He was appointed Papal Secretary of State during the turbulent Protestant Reformation. Charles proved to be very efficient in his subordinate role in the Council of Trent, and became the archbishop of Milan when he was 28 years old. Although his diocese was vast and he was constantly traveling into the remotest villages and Alpine valleys, he persevered and revived Catholicism in Switzerland. His bishopric became the pattern and inspiration of the post-conciliar Church. Charles founded colleges and seminaries, and paid special attention to the discipline and structure of seminaries and priestly training. He took Ambrose as his model. He was St. Aloysius Gonzaga's spiritual father and a friend of St. Philip Neri. A holy and upright bishop who loved his flock, Charles once endured an attempted assassination.

His private life was ascetic and his charity was immense. Two turning points of his life were his eldest brother's death and the plague of 1576-1578. Each spurred him onto more heroic heights of virtue. He ate almost nothing and slept only a few hours, yet his energy was boundless. He wore himself away and died at 46 years of age in 1584. He was canonized in 1610, and is patron of seminarians, catechists, spiritual directors, stomach troubles (especially colic and ulcers), clergy, and apple orchards.

Quote of St. Charles Borromeo:
"If we wish to make progress in the service of God, we must begin every day of our life with new ardor. We must keep ourselves in the presence of God as much as possible and have no other view or end in all our actions but the Divine honor."

Holy Spirit, maintain in Your people that spirit with which You inspired Your Bishop, St. Charles, so that Your Church may be constantly renewed, conforming itself to Christ and manifesting Christ to the world. Amen.

Charlie, Chuck, Carl, Karl, Carol, Caroline, Charlotte, Carlotta, Charlene, Carla

Christ the King

Third Sunday in November

Pilate asked Jesus who had been delivered over to him, "You are then a King?" Jesus responded, "My kingdom is not of this world. If it were, thousands of legions of angels would defend me." His was to be an eternal kingdom subjecting the conscience, mind and will of mankind to the divine law, for "justice and right are the foundation of his throne."

God the Father sent many prophets to herald the coming of His Son, the Savior of mankind. One of these was the Old Testament patriarch, Jacob. On his deathbed, Jacob prophesied about the messianic king who would hold the scepter of Judah. The psalms sing of the blessings of peace in his reign.

Even on this earth we are destined to enjoy a foretaste of his eternal kingdom in heaven. In the Our Father, we pray "Thy Kingdom come. Thy Will be done on earth as it is in heaven." This prayer will be answered when Mary's Immaculate Heart triumphs and the world will be given a wondrous time of peace and love in the Divine Will. She is asking us to prepare for the Eucharistic reign of Jesus through prayer, fasting, and conversion from sin. Just like Jesus and Mary we must "suffer to enter into His glory." Once, Jesus carried the cross to Calvary and died on it, now He carries it like a glorious symbol. The crown of thorns has been transformed into a resplendent crown of glory. "Christ our King, Thy Kingdom come!"

Christ Jesus, I acknowledge You as the King of the Universe. All that has been made has been created for You. Make full use of Your rights over me. I renew the promise I made in Baptism, when I renounced Satan and all his works. I promise to live a Christian life. I, with fervent love, undertake to help to the extent of my means to secure the triumph of the rights of God and his Church. Divine Heart of Jesus, I offer You my poor efforts so that all hearts may acknowledge Your sacred royalty. May the Kingdom of Your peace be established throughout the entire universe. Amen.

Roy, LeRoy, Rexella, Rex (Latin for "king")

St. Daniel

Old Testament Prophet
July 21 ◆ means "divine judge"

Daniel was of the royal blood of the kings of Judah. He, like the rest of his nation, was taken into captivity of Babylon in 586 BC. Since his childhood, Daniel had the spirit of God with him, and for his virtue, uprightness, and wisdom, he was chosen by his captor kings to be their close advisor. God's favor was with Daniel all of his life, and thus he was able to guide the Babylonian rulers and protect his own captive nation by his gift of prophecy and interpretation. Daniel rose to such a high position in the Babylonian kingdom that the jealousy of others provoked them to find a way to make the king despise Daniel. Wicked men persuaded King Darius to secure a law lasting thirty days that forbade anyone to petition anything from another person or god, save the king himself. Daniel, faithful to his prayer to the One, true God, was spied praying. He was brought before King Darius who did not want to punish Daniel, but having to be faithful to the law he decreed, he had Daniel shut up in a den of lions overnight. The king rushed to the cave the next morning to see if Daniel's God had preserved him from the lions. Daniel was miraculously untouched as an angel sent from God protected him. On account of Daniel's gifts, the God of the Hebrews was highly revered by the kings of Babylon. Daniel is the patron of prophets.

On October 5, 2003 St. Daniel Comboni was canonized by Pope John Paul II. He was born in 1831, the sole surviving child of poor parents. Inspired by saintly priests, he discerned a vocation as a Mazza missionary in Africa. In 1864 while praying at St. Peter's Basilica Daniel was inspired to "save the African people with Africans." After setbacks and opposition he founded two colleges and an order of sisters. Because he sheltered fugitive slaves and educated them, he was once abducted in Paris. In 1877 he was consecrated the first bishop of Central Africa. This dynamic multilingual evangelist and rugged explorer contributed also to scholarly journals of geography and ethnology and compiled a Nubian dictionary. On October 10, the feast of another St. Daniel, a missionary martyr, he succumbed to an epidemic and died at age 50. Today 4000 Comboni missionaries courageously carry his love for the poor to mission territories.

Father, may my prayer, like Daniel's, have vital importance in my daily life and nourish my soul's desire and need to be united to You. Amen.

Dan, Danny, Danielle, Dana

St. David

King and Prophet

December 29 ♦ means "beloved"

The prophet Samuel anointed Jesse's youngest son, David, the king of Israel, even while King Saul was still alive. Young David won popularity when he slew Goliath, the Philistine giant, with his slingshot. David rose swiftly through the ranks because of his talents. He became the court musician, and a lieutenant in Saul's army. David's success in battle stirred Saul's jealousy to the extent that he wanted to kill David. David fled to another territory until Saul died, then Israel proclaimed David their king. King David conquered the pagan city of Jerusalem, establishing it as his capitol, and moved the Ark of the Covenant there. Under King David, Israel was victorious over her enemies and flourished culturally. Although God had shown him special favor, David fell into grave sin many times. When he committed adultery with Bathsheba and then killed her husband Uriah, Nathan the prophet rebuked King David. David repented and sought God's forgiveness. David is thought to have written the Psalms, which record his repentance, praise, and love for God. God said of David, "Here is a man after my own heart." He is the patron of poets and musicians.

St. David, "Dewi" in the Welch language, was the son of St. Non and Xantus, an early English prince. After becoming a priest he received spiritual direction from Paulinus, a disciple of St. Germanus. An amazing miracle is attributed to David who cured the aging Paulinus of blindness by making the sign of the cross over him. David built a chapel at Glastonbury, founded 12 monasteries and as an abbot was received by his monks with utter confidence. In a synod he rejected and stifled the spread of the Pelagian heresy in Britain by means of his eloquent speech, intellectual aptitude, and miraculous cures. Finally, as an aged Archbishop of Caerleon and spiritual father of many saints, he died in 544. St. Kentigern saw angels bear his soul to heaven. His feast day is March 1.

The psalms of King David were dearly loved by Archbishop David and his monks.

O God, You have made known Your salvation in the sight of the nations. Your anointed One, Jesus, born of the House of David, rules forever in the Kingdom of God. He comes to reconcile all things in Himself, making peace through the Blood of His Cross. He alone is the alpha and the omega of all that is. Praise be to Jesus Christ, our King. Amen.

Davida, Davine, Dewey, Dewi, Vida, Taffy

St. Deborah

Old Testament Prophetess

means "bee"

Deborah was a prophetess and judge which in essence made her the leader of Israel. Her stature as leader was unusual since Jewish women were stereotyped as being weak and not very wise. Her worthiness to hold such a lofty position is attributed in scripture to her wisdom and strength begotten of the spirit of the Lord. In one account, she summoned General Barak of Israel to convoke 10,000 men to go into battle against General Sisera and the Canaanites. He pleaded for her to go with him and she conceded. She prophesied that the glory of the victory would go partly to a woman which was realized when Sisera was slain by Jahel. Here, two women were chosen by God to confound the strong because they were weak instruments in the powerful Hand of God. Deborah is another prototype of Mary in the battle against evil.

At this time the prophetess Deborah, wife of Laphidoth, was judging Israel. She used to sit under Deborah's palm tree, situated in the mountain region of Ephraim, and there the Israelites came to her for judgment. (Judges 4:4-5)

Canticle of Deborah

When I, Deborah, rose, when I rose, a mother in Israel, new gods were their choice; then the war was at their gates...my heart is with the leaders of Israel, nobles of the people who bless the Lord...sing of them to the strains of the harpers at the wells, where men recount the just deeds of the Lord, his just deeds that brought freedom to Israel. Judges 5:7-11

Debbie, Deb, Debora

St. Denis

Bishop and Martyr
October 9
means "belonging to Dionysius, God of wine"

St. Denis, or Dionysius, was the first bishop of Paris, France. As a zealous bishop, he built a church in Paris and converted a countless number of souls to the faith. St. Denis was imprisoned for a long time. While imprisoned, he and some companions were tortured and finally beheaded in 272 during the reign of the Roman Emperor Valerian. The bodies were thrown into the river Seine, but a pious Christian woman removed the bodies and buried them where they had been beheaded. Legend claims he carried his head accompanied by some singing angels two miles from his place of martyrdom to Saint-Denis; thus is he often portrayed with his head in his hands. In 469, St. Genevieve founded a church over the burial place. In the seventh century, a great abbey was added to the location and became the burial place of the French kings. This area now is called Saint-Denis. St. Denis is the patron of France, and is invoked against demons and frenzie. He is one of the original fourteen Holy Helpers.

Quote of St. Denis:
"Of all divine things, the most Godlike is to cooperate with God in the conversion of sinners."

Commemoration from his Mass

O God, who for the enduring of his passing did on this day endow blessed Denis, Thy martyr and bishop, with the virtue of constancy and who for the preaching of the glory to the heathen did appoint Rusticus and Eleutherius as his fellow workers' grant that we may follow their example of mortification for the sake of thy love and by not fearing any adversities. Amen.

Lord, increase the zeal of all the bishops so that they, like Saint Denis, will have the courage to serve their flocks faithfully even at the cost of their own lives. Amen.

Dion, Denny, Denise, Denine

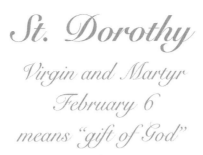

St. Dorothy

Virgin and Martyr
February 6
means "gift of God"

Dorothy grew up in Asia Minor. Fabritius, the governor of Caesarea, tortured this young girl because she refused to adore false gods or marry. Two wicked ladies were sent to seduce her, but she remained steadfast in her faith and converted them. It is also said that she converted a judge named Theophilus when she gave him fruits and flowers that were miraculously obtained from her divine Spouse. In the flower of her youth, she was beheaded for her unshakable faith in Jesus at Caesarea in Cappadocia in 311 under Emperor Diocletian. Her remains are kept in the church of St. Dorothy in Rome beyond the Tiber River. She is the patroness of gardeners and newlyweds.

Dear St. Dorothy, since you are the patron of gardeners and newlyweds, pray that all married couples may see marriage as a spiritual garden ready to sprout and bloom according to God's glorious Will. Newlyweds are privileged initiators, procreators with the Creator. The life or loves they bring about through conception or acquire through adoption - like potted plants from a garden nursery and then nurture - are destined to bloom for all eternity. While some will have their own children or adopt, other couples will be fruitful in a higher realm only, the spiritual, of course, the most important of all, like St. Henry and St. Cunegundes and like St. Juan Diego and his wife Maria, St. Catherine of Genoa and her husband, and many more. May we all meet you in God's heavenly garden of souls, rejoicing in all the life, goodness, and love marriage has brought about.

Loving Lord, inspire in all youth the desire to defend and protect the flower of their purity in word, thought, and action. May they never defile their bodies, the living temples of the Holy Spirit. Amen.

Dora, Dot, Dorie, Dorothea, Dolly, Doreen

St. Edward

Edward was born in England, but at the age of ten he and his brother Alfred were sent for safety to Normandy and grew up there. His brother returned to England and was believed to have been murdered by Edward's future father-in-law. Edward became King of England at the age of forty in 1042. Once a king, he married a noblewoman named Edith so that the people of England would have a queen. Nonetheless, since he had vowed his virginity to the Blessed Virgin Mary, he and Queen Edith lived as brother and sister. England flourished under his reign; he restored Westminster Abbey, and rebuilt old churches that had fallen into ruin. Edward personally cared for and miraculously cured the poor, sick, and lepers. He was called "Good King Edward" for he was so holy, kind, and generous that a ring he gave to a beggar was returned to him by St. John the Evangelist with a warning of speedy death and then Paradise. His interest in hunting never interfered with his daily attendance of Holy Mass. King Edward died in 1066. He is the patron of hunters. Of known English saints, his body alone rests in the Westminster Abbey.

There is another St. Edward the Martyr whose feast day is March 18. He was baptized by St. Dunstan, the Archbishop of Canterbury. He was crowned King of England as a youth and three years later murdered by his younger brother's retainers in order to over throw the throne. His body was found in a marsh because a pillar of light shone upon it. Thereafter miracles took place at his tomb.

O God, may St. Edward's noble and generous heart be a model for all the nations' rulers so that they see clearly that their mission is to establish peace and harmony among Your people. Amen.

Ed, Ted, Ned, Eduardo, Edna

St. Elizabeth of Hungary

Widow and Queen
November 17
means "worshipper of God"

At four years of age, Elizabeth, the daughter of the king of Hungary, went to the Thuringian court to be raised and married to Ludwig of Thuringia. They were happily married when she was fifteen and he was twenty. Although she was a queen, she refused to wear her crown in the chapel and would rise from bed at night to pray. She cared for the sick and the poor daily, often selling her clothes and jewelry to do so, and then wearing simple undyed garments under her cape as shown in the picture. She constructed a hospital near the palace. Ludwig died on a Holy Land crusade, leaving Elizabeth a widow and mother at the age of twenty. She and her three children were exiled by a power-thirsty brother-in-law, but soon after she was returned to her rightful position. Elizabeth became a Third-Order Franciscan and continued her charitable works. She died in 1302, when she was only twenty-four. Germans still call her their "Dear St. Elizabeth." Her husband was beatified and is called "Blessed Ludwig."

St. Elizabeth of Portugal was named after her aunt St. Elizabeth of Hungary. She owed her rapid climb to sanctity to early spiritual training which taught her the virtue of obedience and submission to God's Will. She also learned to be considerate of others for love of God. Parents who excite the willfulness and self-indulgence of their children by teaching them a love of worthless things and giving into every whim and want would do well to consider this. When twelve she married the King of Portugal who was a good ruler but selfish and unfaithful in private life. She treated him with cheerful and patient love. Problems arose between their son and the illegitimate sons of the king, and "Elizabeth the Peacemaker" even rode out and stopped a battle in her old age.

Quote of St. Elizabeth:
"I want to be able to say to Jesus, "Jesus, when You were hungry, I gave You to eat. When You were naked, I clothed You. When You were sick, I visited You."

Heavenly Father, teach us through St. Elizabeth's example how to generously serve You in the poor and sick we meet throughout our lives. Amen.

Betsy, Betty, Liz, Lisa, Bess, Eliza, Liza, Beth, Libby, Lillian, Isabel, Elsie, Gisella

St. Fiacre

Between 600 and 670, an Irish missionary named Fiacre was welcomed by St. Faro, Bishop of Meaux, to set up a hermitage in one of the most fertile districts in France. So many pilgrims sought him out that he had to clear more land near his oratory for the construction of a hospice. He also gardened to feed them and cared for the sick. However, women were not allowed within the enclosure as "spunky" ones soon found out, and even suffered strange maladies for their disrespect.

Louis XIII's wife Queen Anne prayed humbly outside the door of St. Fiacre's hermitage for her dangerously ill husband because it was known that miracles happened through the intercession of this great saint. By means of the prayer of Queen Anne and the intercession of St. Fiacre, Louis XIII was miraculously healed. Among the many answers to prayers for the royal couple, a very important answered prayer was the safe delivery of little Louis who would later be King Louis XIV. The first Parisian cabs were called "fiacres" because they brought many pilgrims from St. Fiacre's Hotel to his shrine in La Brie on the first stage of their journey.

St. Fiacre is the patron of gardeners, tile-makers, potters, Parisian cab-drivers, hemorrhoids, and venereal disease.

Dear Patron of gardeners, tile makers, potters, and et cetera help us to help others with our talents for love of the eternal Father, prayerfully bringing forth food and beauty to nourish and cheer his often sick and weary children, our brothers and sisters. Together with you we ask this through Jesus Christ Our lord. Amen.

Lord Jesus, help me to appreciate silence and seclusion as opportunities for me to speak to You just as St. Fiacre drew his holiness and happiness from You in silence and solitude. Amen.

St. Francis of Assisi

Francis was born into a wealthy and renowned family in Assisi, Italy in 1182. His father was a successful merchant who wished Francis to follow in his footsteps. Francis, however, liked to have excitement and fun, and his dreams were fulfilled when he joined a crusade as a knight. Injured in battle, Francis was sent home and confined to bed during which time he underwent a conversion having heard the Lord calling him to follow Him. Francis had a vision at the church of San Damiano in which Jesus, speaking from the crucifix, told him: "Build my Church." Francis was moved to embrace poverty in a special way, and began to appreciate and love God's creation. He exchanged his fine clothes for shepherd's rags that enraged his father. Other men gathered around Francis because of his joyful personality and contagious love for God. This following obliged Francis to seek the Pope's approval to begin the Franciscan Order. Francis ardently desired to travel to the East to be martyred by the Moors, but instead they made friends with him. He also received the stigmata (the wounds of Christ), and lived a life so austere that at the age of 44 his body weakened and he died October 4, 1226. St. Francis is the patron of Catholic action and also of animals.

Prayer of St. Francis: "Lord, make me an instrument of Your peace. Where there is hatred - let me sow love. Where there is doubt - let me sow faith. Where there is despair - hope. Where there is darkness - light. Where there is sadness - joy. O Divine Master, grant that I may not so much seek to be consoled - as to console; to be understood - as to understand; to be loved - as to love. For it is in giving that we receive; it is in pardoning that we are pardoned. And it is in dying that we are born to eternal life. Amen."

Quotes of St. Francis:
"Alms are an inheritance and a justice which is due to the poor, and which Jesus Christ has levied upon us."
"Even though I had committed but one little sin, I should have ample reason to repent of it all my life."

O God, You enabled St. Francis to imitate Christ by his poverty and humility. Walking in St. Francis' footsteps, may we follow Your Son and be bound to You by a joyful love. Amen.

Franklin, Frank, Franz, Fran, Francesco, Francois, Frances, Francine

St. Francis Xavier

Co-founder of Jesuits, Missionary
December 3
Co-founder
means "free", "fascinating"

Francis was born 1506 to a noble Spanish family and in time became a worldly student at the University of Paris, but he could not resist the call of Christ through a fellow student, St. Ignatius of Loyola. He became one of Ignatius' Jesuit co-founders on August 15, 1534, the feast of Our Lady's Assumption. Ignatius chose Francis to be the first Jesuit missionary of India. Consumed by zeal for his faith, Francis traveled throughout and beyond India preaching the love of God. In Japan, he won 400,000 souls for Christ. Francis was betrayed by the captain of the ship on his way to China and left on an island. There he died of a fever in a tiny shack with one companion on December 3, 1552 before he could fulfill his dream of preaching in China. His body is incorrupt.

St. Francis Xavier is an astounding example of the maxim of his mentor, Ignatius: "Few souls understand what God would accomplish in them if they were to abandon themselves unreservedly to Him and if they were to allow His grace to mould them accordingly." He is the patron saint of foreign missions, apostolates of prayer, winemakers, hospital administrators, Australia, Borneo, China, New Zealand, and immigrants, and emigrants.

Dear St. Francis, although I may not travel across the world to preach Christ to others, teach me how to preach Christ everyday, wherever I am, through my words and actions. Amen.

Frank, Franz, Francine, Frances, Fritz, Francette, Xavier

St. Gabriel

Archangel
September 29
means "strength of God"

Gabriel is the angelic messenger. When God has news to announce, we see throughout the bible that it is St. Gabriel the archangel who is sent to speak for God to His people. St. Gabriel announced the coming of the Messiah to the prophet Daniel in the Old Testament. St. Gabriel was also sent to bear the good news to Zachary that he and Elizabeth would have the child who would prepare the way for Jesus Christ, St. John the Baptist. The most beautiful news St. Gabriel had to announce was to the Blessed Virgin Mary. His words compose the first verses of the Hail Mary: "Hail, Mary, full of grace. The Lord is with you." She was chosen to be the Mother of God, and he enjoyed the honor of hearing the fiat from her sweet lips. Some Church Fathers say that St. Gabriel was the angel who consoled Jesus in the Garden of Gethsemane. St. Gabriel is the Angel of the Incarnation, consolation, joy, and mercy. He is also the patron of communication workers.

A saint bearing the same name as the Archangel, Gabriel of Our Lady of Sorrow, died as a model of youth at the age of 24. There is one noteworthy worldly trait of his though; he was an excellent marksman, actually saving the town from attack by a quick demonstration with a gun. Gabriel was extraordinary in the way that he simply and faithfully followed the vocation which called him to detachment and total self-giving to God. He became a Passionist who learned to love Christ's passion and became ardently devoted to the Sorrowful Mother. He was canonized in 1920. Like his namesake, he was very close to Our Lady, as those who bear the name Gabriel are meant to be.

O Jesus, form the ranks of all the angels You chose the Archangel Gabriel to announce the mystery of Your Incarnation. Grant that we, who honor him on earth, may experience the effect of his patronage in heaven. Amen.

Gabe, Gabrielle, Gabriela, Gabby

St. Genesius

Martyr, Comedian
August 25

The real Genesius was only a court clerk who no longer wished to be an accomplice in the killing of Christians. This conversion earned for him a glorious martyrdom. A legend grew around him that is a beautifully woven tale: Genesius was a renowned comedian and the head of a theatrical group in the Roman Empire in the 4th Century. One day he was performing for the Roman Emperor in Rome. Part of the routine included a skit mocking the Christian sacrament of baptism. As Genesius was playing the part of the candidate for the sacrament, he approached the other actor who was impersonating the priest. Following the script, the priest actor asked Genesius, "Well, my child, why has thou sent for me?" In that moment, the heathen Genesius received the grace of conversion. He responded honestly, "I desire to receive the grace of Jesus Christ and to be relieved from the weight of my sins, which oppress me." His fellow actor continued the scene by pouring water over his head. Genesius had a vision of an angel who held a book of the comedian's sins, who immersed the book in the waters of baptism, making it white. As the act played on, Genesius was dressed in the white robe of a neophyte and apprehended by the soldiers who brought him before the emperor. At this point, no one knew that Genesius was no longer acting. Genesius broke his role and professed himself a Christian before the emperor. The emperor thought he was still acting, but when he saw the actor's truthfulness, he was infuriated and ordered him to be beaten with clubs and then tortured so that he might deny Christ. Before being beheaded, Genesius said, "All possible tortures shall never take Jesus Christ from my heart or from my lips. My only grief is that I have so long persecuted His holy name, and have learned to adore Him so late." Genesius was martyred between the years 285 and 303. He is the patron saint of notaries, actors, dancers, mountebanks, freezing, and epilepsy.

Merciful God, You gave Genesius the grace of conversion. As sinners, may none of us ever pass up the grace of conversion in our lives, but rather respond to Your call to come home to You. Amen.

St. Genevieve

Virgin

January 3

means "humble birth"

Genevieve was born near Paris around the year 422. When she was seven years old, St. Germanus, a French bishop, prophesied the child's future sanctity to her parents. He received her consecration to God. Her mother, who would not allow the child to attend Mass, suffered blindness for a time as a result of her stubbornness against God's Will. Genevieve lived her life as a shepherdess. At the age of 15, she donned the virgin's veil from St. Germanus as an external sign of her consecration to God. Her call to live an austere life is evident by her custom of eating only two days a week. On these days she would merely eat barley bread and beans. She had the power to heal and to prophesy, however, some people began to gossip about her and even wanted to drown her. In 448, God saw fit to remove this reproach; after St. Germanus showed his approval of her, Genevieve's enemies turned their calumny and suspicion into veneration and admiration. Genevieve did much to save her people from the Franks who invaded Gaul. She herself managed to bring shiploads of corn when famine broke out. Through fasting and prayer she helped divert Attila the Hun who planned to march on Paris. Genevieve played a pivotal role in the construction of the great basilica of St. Denis in which her body is now buried; she encouraged and miraculously supplied wine to the building crew, thereby securing its construction.

Genevieve died in the year 500. In art, Genevieve is typically shown with a lit candle in her hand.

O Mighty God, You found St. Genevieve's prayer and fasting worthy to stop disaster. Open the hearts of Your faithful so that we turn to fasting and prayer to win Your favor and obtain Your help in those moments that we feel powerless. Amen.

Gen, Genny

St. Godfrey of Amiens

Bishop and Confessor

November 8

means "at peace with God"

Five-year-old Godfrey was entrusted to the care of the abbot of Mont-Saint Quentin. In due course he became a monk, was ordained, became a holy abbot, and then was named bishop of Amiens in 1104. If Bishop Godfrey thought the cook was treating him too well, he would order that his portion of food be given to the poor or sick, for he lived in the simplest fashion.

In his diocese, Godfrey struggled against simony and promoted the celibacy of the clergy, in the course of which an attempt was made on his life by a disgruntled woman. He was inflexibly just; and his rigid discipline was very unpopular among the less worthy. Terribly discouraged by secular pressures, he wanted to resign and join the Carthusians. In November of 1115, he died while traveling toward Soissens and was buried there.

The name Godfrey or Jeffrey is connected with the Holy Shroud of Turin on its journey though history from the Holy Sepulcher to Turin. For about 150 years it was secretly safe guarded by the Knights Templar who vowed poverty, chastity and obedience. Their honesty was unquestioned and they were often entrusted with valuables including relics. In the 1350s one of these knights Geoffrey de Charny emerged as the owner of the Holy Shroud. His son Geoffrey inherited it later and it passed on again.

St. Godfrey's life seemed to roll smoothly and successfully along until he was ordained bishop. This was a heavy cross for him. To him we can pray for intercession from God for our bishops, that they may endure in their heroic struggle to lead their flocks safely through the perils of our times. St. Godfrey, pray for us!

Geoffrey, Geof, Jeffrey, Jeff

The Good Shepherd
The Fourth Sunday of Easter

The image of the Good Shepherd illustrates Jesus' personal and sacrificial love for us, the sheep of His flock. The loving Shepherd knows His sheep and they know Him. Jesus guides us with His staff, guards us from the enemy who wishes to devour us and nourishes us with His very own Body and Blood-the Eucharist. As He promises in John 10, He never leaves His flock untended, but instead gives us His Church and His Eucharist to guide and strengthen us on our journey to Heaven.

"The Lord is my Shepherd; there is nothing I shall want. He gives me rest in fresh green pastures. He leads me near restful waters to restore my drooping spirit. If I should walk in the shadow of darkness, no evil shall I fear. You are there with the strength of Your staff, which gives me Your comfort." Psalm 22:1-4

"We are all both sheep and shepherd; we are Christ's sheep and, in one way and another, in our turn, shepherds of His sheep." St. Augustine

"At that time Jesus said to the Pharisees: "I am the good shepherd. The good shepherd gives his life for his sheep. But the hireling, and he that is not the shepherd, whose own the sheep are not, sees the wolf coming and leaves the sheep and flees: and the wolf catches and scatters the sheep: and the hireling flees because he is hired and has no care for the sheep. I am the good shepherd and care for my sheep. I am the good shepherd: and I know Mine, and Mine know Me, as the Father knows me, and I know the Father, and I lay down My life for my sheep. And other sheep I have that are not of the fold. Them also I must bring, and they shall hear my voice, and there shall be one fold and one shepherd." John 10:11-16

St. Gregory the Great

Pope and Doctor of the Church
September 3
means "watchful"

Gregory was born into a pious and patristic family in Italy in 540. His mother was St. Sylvia. Gregory received an excellent education that prepared him to hold the highest political position as Prefect of Rome at the age of 30. He fulfilled his career honorably and honestly. He left behind the world and his wealth to follow God in the monastic life. Gregory turned his home into a monastery, but being highly talented, he was called out of monastic life several times to fulfill lofty positions. When the pope died from the plague in 590, the people unanimously elected Gregory to be pope. Gregory's pastoral task was not easy. He had to confront the onslaught of barbarian invasions. When political efforts failed to quell the Lombards' thirst for land and power in 593, Gregory convinced Agilulf and his army to leave Rome in peace. One of Gregory's greatest achievements and his favorite accomplishment was the evangelization of England. There he saved many slaves, and converted them for Christ. Gregory composed the first music of the Church, the Gregorian chant. His commentaries on sacred Scripture and other writings greatly influenced Christian thought in the Middle Ages and won him a place with St. Ambrose, St. Augustine and St. Jerome as one of the four great Doctors of the Latin Church. He is the patron of popes, school children, and singers, especially choirboys. He died March 12, 604.

Quote of St. Gregory:
"The sick are to realize that they are sons of God by the very fact that the scourge of discipline chastises them. For unless it were His plan to give them an inheritance after their chastisements, He would not trouble to school them in afflictions."

O God, through the intercession of Pope St. Gregory, give wisdom to the leaders of Your Church that the growth of Your people in holiness may be the everlasting joy of our pastors. Amen.

Craig, Greg, Sylvia

Guardian Angels
October 2

Out of a personal and unique love, God created angels to protect and guide His creatures. St. Paul tells us that the mission of the angels is to protect the future heirs of salvation.

Each angel has its specific mission and charge. At the moment of our birth, we receive our guardian angel, and this angel remains faithfully at our side, comforts us in purgatory, and then escorts us to Heaven. Besides giving each person his or her own angel, God has designated an angel for each nation, country, kingdom, church, and religious order. Catholic bishops have two angels, and the Holy Father has special angels to help him fulfill his task as Christ's vicar on earth. Many saints have seen their guardian angels. St. Frances of Rome saw hers constantly. Out of shame, he would hide his face or fade away when she sinned or committed a fault. St. Augustine wrote, "Go where we will, our angels are always with us." St. Bernard says, "Make the holy angels your friends. No matter how weak we may be, or lowly our condition, or how great the dangers which surround us, we have nothing to fear under the protection of these guardians."

There are nine choirs of angels:

Angel	Guardian angels
Archangels	Seven of these are very special (Michael, Gabriel, Raphael, Uriel, Jehudiel, Sealtiel and Barachiel)
Virtues	Guardians of the virtues in souls
Powers	Special choir for priests
Principalities	Guardians of churches, dioceses and provinces
Dominions	Guardians to inspire teachers of religion
Thrones	Guardians of seminaries
Cherubim	Protectors of shrines, sanctuaries, and the Holy Father
Seraphim	Totally absorbed in love and adoration of God before His throne

Angel of God, my guardian dear, to whom His love commits me here. Ever this day, be at my side to light, to guard, to rule and guide. From sinful stain, O keep me free, and in my hour of death, my helper be. Amen.

Angel, Angela, Angeline, Angie, Angelica

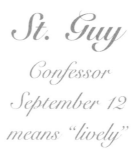

St. Guy

Confessor
September 12
means "lively"

St. Guy, the "Poor Man of Anderlecht," was a simple, hidden soul born of poor peasants who valued the spiritual. In spite of Guy's lack of education and money, he learned to be content, even happy to be deprived. He fasted that he might be able to help the poor. His goodness enabled him to be chosen as a sacristan for the church of Our Lady at Lacken near Brussels, Belgium. The order and cleanliness of everything under his direction drew constant compliments from all who enter the church. With his small savings, Guy left his work as a sacristan and he entered into a partnership with a merchant who claimed Guy could do more for the poor on the profit from a commercial venture. The ship of goods was lost at sea, and Guy was left penniless and unemployed. He became a pilgrim in reparation and traveled to Rome and the Holy Land. Worn out by seven years of hardships and illness, Guy returned to Anderlecht, even then assisting another pilgrim, and died at a hospital there in 1012. Such miracles took place at his grave that his body was translated into a shrine. He is the patron of sacristans and those who work with horses. He is also known as St. Wye or Guidon.

Dear St. Guy, in your zeal to better help the poor you became a partner in a venture that failed and cost you your job as a sacristan. Then you wore yourself out as a poor pilgrim in reparation. Pray for us in the vicissitudes of life which you knew so well that we may simply and humbly accept God's will and finally come to join you and all the saints praising God forever. Amen.

Guido, Vitus, Wye, Guidon

St. Henry

Henry was born in 972 to a royal family. He was the Duke of Bavaria when he married St. Cunegunda of Luxemburg. Together they lived in celibacy. He had to accept God's Will for him and became the Holy Roman Emperor and a great benefactor for the Benedictines. He enjoyed building and restoring Benedictine monasteries. With the encouragement of his wife, he founded the great cathedral at Bamberg. He died at the age of 52 in 1024 having ruled for 22 years. Henry was prudent, courageous, and merciful, a great model for Christian kings. Like Jacob, the patriarch of the Old Testament, he was injured in the sinew of the leg and made lame. The Great King of the Apocalypse will also be lame. In the 20th century, St. Pius X declared St. Henry the patron of Finland and of all the Oblates of the Benedictine Order.

Lord, like St. Henry, may world leaders take upon themselves the mission of rebuilding the Church of Christ Your Son for the future generations so that Your Kingdom is extended here on earth. Amen.

Hal, Harry, Enrique, Heinz, Hank, Henrietta, Hattie, Retta, Nettien, Harriet

St. Cunegunda

St. Cunegunda of Luxemburg married St. Henry, Duke of Bavaria. However, Cunegunda was accused by certain calumniators of liberties with other men. She knew this scandal must be stopped so she cleared herself by oath and the ordeal trials by walking over 12 heated plough shares without hurt. When her husband died, Cunegunda joined the Benedictine nuns. From the moment of her consecration to God, she seemed to forget that she was formerly an empress and became the humblest servant in the convent she had founded. She died March 3, 1033 or 1039.

Jesus, through St. Cunegunda's intercession, may all women feel inspired to be exemplary in their humility, purity, femininity, and strength. Amen.

The Holy Eucharist
Feast of Corpus Christi in June

What distinguishes the Roman Catholic faith from others is the belief in Jesus' real presence, Body, Blood, Soul, and Divinity in the Eucharist. Catholics believe Jesus is present at the moment of consecration during Holy Mass (the moment in which the priest repeats the words of Jesus on Holy Thursday and the bread and wine truly become the Body and Blood of our Savior) and in the tabernacle when He is reserved there. He waits for us to come to adore Him, speak with Him, and seek His counsel near His presence in the tabernacle. Jesus promised that He would be with us until the end of the world, and the Eucharist is how He keeps this promise. The Church established the annual feast day of Corpus Christi in June so that we give thanks for the gift of the Eucharist.

"Humans aim, by means of food and drink, not to be hungry or thirsty anymore, but they can only attain this state through that unique food and drink which makes those who receive it steadfast and incorruptible. In this way is formed the Communion of Saints, where peace and perfect unity are found; therefore Our Lord in leaving us His Body and Blood, chose for this purpose substances, the unity of which is composed of several parts, one single loaf made of many grains of wheat; one kind of wine formed from the mingled juice of many grapes." Third Nocturne ~ St. Augustine

"Why do we permit our souls to die of thirst when the Fountain of Living Water is just around the corner?" Mother Angelica

"Jesus is there in the tabernacle expressly for you...for you alone. He burns with the desire to come into your heart!" St. Therese of Lisieux

Lord Jesus Christ, You gave us the Eucharist as a memorial of Your suffering and death. May our worship of this Sacrament of Your Body and Blood help us to experience the salvation You won for us and the peace of the Kingdom where You live forever. Amen

The Holy Family
First Sunday after Christmas

Jesus, the Virgin Mary, and Joseph, were united by God the Father's loving design to form the Holy Family. Jesus, the eternal Word made flesh, is the center of and reason for this union of persons. Mary serves as Jesus' pure mother who obediently cooperated with God's grace so that Jesus would share in our humanity. Joseph served as Jesus' foster father and protector of Mary's virginity. Together they mirror the perfect family life where all members are united and centered around Jesus Christ, and there is exercised profound respect and love between the spouses and towards the children. Jesus, Mary, and Joseph as the Holy Family are patrons of Christian family life.

O God of goodness and mercy, to Thy fatherly guidance we commend our family, Your household and all our belongings. We commit all to Thy love and keeping; do Thou fill this house with Thy blessings even as Thou didst fill the Holy House of Nazareth with Thy presence. Amen

Protect us and our house from all evils and misfortunes but grant that we may ever be resigned to Thy divine Will even in our sorrows. Finally give us the grace of perfect harmony and fullness of love for our neighbor. Grant that all of us may deserve by a holy life the comfort of the last Sacraments at the hour of death. O Jesus, bless and protect us. Amen.

Lord Jesus Christ, Who, being made subject to Mary and Joseph, consecrated domestic life by Thy ineffable virtues; grant that we, with the assistance of both, may be taught by the example of Thy Holy Family and may attain to its everlasting fellowship. Amen.

Your home was a garden,
Made glad with fairest flowers;
May life thus blossom sweetly
In every home of ours.
~from an old hymn

St. Hubert

Little is known of Hubert's early life. Accounts reveal that he was strongly addicted to hunting and to worldly pursuits. One legend about the saint explains that while hunting, Hubert saw a brilliant cross appear suspended between the antlers of a buck. This sign inspired him to consider the priesthood. Witnessing Hubert's holy virtue and aptitude for learning, St. Lambert, Bishop of Maestricht, ordained him a priest. St. Lambert was murdered in 681, and Hubert was chosen his successor. He evangelized the barbarians in Ardenne, and strove to eliminate idol worship. God granted him the gift of performing miracles. He died May 30, 727, with the Our Father and the Creed on his lips. St. Hubert is the patron saint of hunters, those who care for dogs, and those who suffer hydrophobia.

St. Andrew Hubert Fournet ◆ May 13

After an idle and frivolous childhood of frequent scrapes, his family sent him to a holy uncle, a priest serving a poverty stricken parish. In his school book now preserved as a relic, Andrew wrote, "This book belongs to Andrew Hubert Fournet, a good boy, though he is not going to be a priest or a monk!" His uncle's humility and love inspired Andrew to respond to God's call for him to be a priest. After ordination he served as his uncle's curate and eventually he became the priest of his hometown. Living in his ancestral home, now his rectory, Andrew gave all but the necessities away and embraced a life of simplicity in action and speech. His charity and winning personality endeared him to all.

When the French Revolution arose, priests who refused to take an oath were outlawed. Knowing he could suffer if caught, Andrew continued to take care of his flock in hiding. On one occasion, a woman, protecting Andrew from being arrested, boxed him on the ears in order to offer the police a fireside seat. She then sent him out to mind the cattle as though he was a hired hand. Andrew said later "She had a heavy hand. She made me see stars!" In 1834 he died at 82 years old.

Holy Spirit, many times my personal interests and pleasures take me away from devoting myself more to my faith. May I discover Your presence, graciousness, and love in creating wholesome hobbies and interests for me to enjoy. Amen.

Infant of Prague

The valuable statue of the Infant Jesus was brought to Bohemia by a Spanish princess, Maria Manriques as a gift from her mother on the occasion of her marriage to a Czech nobleman. She gave it as a wedding gift again to her daughter Polyzena. When Polyzena became a widow, she donated the Infant to the Carmelites in Prague saying, "I hereby give you what I prize most highly in this world. As long as you venerate this image, you will not be in want." Their hardship ceased and the community prospered.

Venerable Cyril of the Mother of God was delivered of severe interior trials by prayers to the miraculous Infant. Things went badly after Brother Cyril and the novices had to leave, since the statue was no longer honored and even thrown out on a heap of rubbish during the Thirty Years War. For seven years the statue was buried in rubble. On the feast of Pentecost Father Cyril now ordained, returned and the community was in distress till he remembered the promise of prosperity connected with devotion to the Holy Infant. He searched for and found the waxed wooden statue buried in debris, its hands missing. One day as he was praying, he heard the words distinctly, "Have pity on Me, and I will have pity on you. Give Me My hands, and I will give you peace. The more you honor Me, the more I will bless you." So they replaced it with a new Infant statue that was shattered immediately by a falling candlestick. The original was finally repaired and the Holy Infant was evidently pleased. Such were the heavenly favors procured, that replicas had to be made and sent everywhere.

Pope Leo XIII confirmed the devotion of the Infant of Prague in 1896 favoring it with many indulgences.

O Jesus King, we crown Thee with diadem most fair. O'er all Thou reignest solely. Thy might is everywhere. With pride we tell Thy story, O wondrous Babe of Prague! With joy we sing Thy glory, O little King of Prague! Amen

"The more you honor Me, the more I will bless you." Amen

St. Irene

Virgin and Martyr
April 3
means "peaceful"

St. Irene was apprehended in 304, after the decree of Diocletian in 303 declared the possession of sacred Christian writings punishable by death. Irene, a daughter of pagan parents, lived in Thessalonica in Macedonia with her two Christian sisters, Agape and Chionia. Arrested upon another charge, these sisters' volumes of Holy Scripture were not discovered or known to exist by anyone else until a year after their arrest. The following charge was read during the trial: "The Pensioner Cassander to Dulcitius, President of Macedonia, greetings. I send to your Highness six Christian women and one man who refused to eat meat sacrificed to the gods. Their names are Agape, Chionia, Irene, Cassian, Philippa, and Eutychia, and the man is called Agatho." The governor, in turn, asked each Christian his or her response to the charge. When he asked Irene why she did not comply with the custom, she bravely replied, "Because I was afraid of offending God." Irene's sisters, Agape and Chionia were burnt alive for disobeying Roman law. Irene, however, was called a second time before the governor, and again, she refused to worship the gods, even though such an act would save her life. Irene was condemned to death. Her suffering was more intense and prolonged than that of her sisters. She was stripped and on view in a house of ill repute, yet God would not allow His virgin to undergo the slightest molestation. Afterwards, Irene was put to death by being burnt at the stake or shot in the throat by an arrow.

O God, St. Irene and her noble sisters teach me how I should revere the Word of God. They suffered when they could not satisfy the longing they had to openly and freely read Scripture. Instill in me profound gratitude for this freedom I have. Amen.

Irena, Irenea

St. Jacob

Patriarch

August 28

means "supplanter"

Jacob was the son of Isaac and Rebecca. With his mother's aid he obtained Isaac's blessing and the birthright instead of his older brother, Esau. Following his mother's advice, Jacob stayed with his uncle Laban to escape Esau's revenge. As he was traveling across the desert, Jacob grew tired and slept with his head upon a rock. He saw in his sleep a ladder standing upon the earth, its top touching heaven. Angels of God ascended and descended the ladder and the Lord leant upon it saying to Jacob, "I am the Lord God of Abraham your father, and the God of Isaac; the land, wherein you sleep, I will give to you and to your seed." The Lord promised Jacob many descendants and assured Jacob that He Himself would be his Protector and remain with him always. Jacob rose from his slumber and praised God for the marvels he had done for His chosen people. After Jacob wrestled with an angel, God named Jacob 'Israel' meaning, "one who wrestled with an angel." His sons through Leah and Rachel were the fathers of the twelve tribes of Israel.

During the widespread famine in Palestine Jacob and his eleven sons were welcomed to live in Egypt by Joseph, the favorite son whom Jacob had mourned for many years as dead. On his deathbed Jacob prophesied for each of his sons but especially for Juda, "The scepter shall not be taken from Juda, nor a ruler from his thigh, till he comes who is to be sent, and he shall be the expectation of nations." This Messianic king is Jesus, Son of God. Jacob's bones were buried in the promised land.

Heavenly Father, Your mercy extends to every generation. Let us see with faith all the good and marvelous works You wish to realize in the lives of those who want to live as Your children. Amen.

Jay, Jake, Jacoba, Coby, Jacqueline

St. James the Greater

Apostle and Martyr

July 25

means "supplanter"

Jesus called James and his brother John on the shore of Tiberius. He named them the "Sons of Thunder" probably on account of their fiery and energetic personalities. When these two brothers saw Jesus the first time, they followed behind Him until He turned around and asked, "What do you want?" They replied, "Master, we want to know where you live." Jesus invited them to "Come and see." Thus began their friendship with Christ. Throughout His public ministry, Jesus showed these brothers and Peter a special love by having them present on certain occasions that the other disciples were not at: the Transfiguration and the agony in the Garden of Gethsemane. After Jesus ascended into heaven, St. James is thought to have gone to Spain to evangelize. Compostela in Northern Spain has a cathedral dedicated to St. James, and was a very popular place of pilgrimage for all of Europe in the middle Ages. There is a beautiful legend of a statue of Our Lady of the Pillar in the Cathedral of St. James at Saragossa, Spain. Legend has it that Mary was carried on a throne from Jerusalem to Spain by the Holy Angels who sang beautiful hymns and carved this statue and pillar. Mary told James that Jesus wanted him to come back to Jerusalem where he would be martyred for His sake. He returned to Jerusalem and was killed under Herod about 43 AD, making him the first of the twelve apostles to die for Christ. He is the patron of arthritics, pharmacists, and those who suffer from rheumatism. His feast day is celebrated with great festivity in Spain and Chile.

Almighty and ever-living God, through the blood of St. James You consecrated the first fruits of the ministry of Your Apostles. Grant that Your Church may be strengthened by his confession and always enjoy his patronage. Amen.

Jay, Diego, Yakov, Jim, Jamie, Jaime, Jayma

St. Jane Frances de Chantal

Widow and Abbess
December 12
means "the Lord's grace", "free"

Jane Frances was born in France in 1582. Her father was the president of the French Parliament of Burgundy. When she was twenty years old her father arranged for her to marry the Baron of Chantal, who was relative of St. Bernard. Her good and devoted husband died in a hunting accident, leaving the twenty-eight year old Jane Frances with a son and three daughters. Urged to marry again, she felt called to remain single, and raised her children as a single parent. After having raised her children to adulthood, she entered the convent which grieved her children very much because they couldn't see her as often as they would have liked. St. Jane Frances' life was not without suffering for she lost her own sister, a daughter, and her only son in a war. Although she suffered, she served God faithfully through every trial. Under the direction of her spiritual guide, St. Francis de Sales, she founded the Visitation Order in 1610. St. Vincent de Paul said of Jane Frances: "She was full of faith, and yet all her life long she had been tormented by thoughts against it. Nor did she once relax in the fidelity God asked of her. And so I regard her as one of the holiest souls I have ever met on this earth." St. Jane Frances died December 12, 1641, at the age of sixty-nine. She is the patron of prayer and contemplation.

Quotes of St. Jane Frances de Chantal:
"The great method of prayer is to have none. If, in going to prayer one can form in oneself a pure capacity for receiving the Spirit of God, that will suffice for all method."
"In our neighbors we should observe only what is good."

O God, You endowed St. Jane Frances with admirable qualities in various walks of life. Through her intercession help us to be true to our vocation and never fail to bear witness to the light You give us. Amen.

Janie, Joan, Jean, Jeanne, Janet, Johanna, Joanna, Jessica

St. Jason

Martyr
July 12
means, "healing"

A prominent citizen of the city of Salonika named Jason received St. Paul and Silas as guests in his home. In consequence of Paul's successful preaching there, the Jews "moved with envy and taking unto them some wicked men of the vulgar sort, and making a tumult, set the city in an uproar; and besetting Jason's house sought to bring them out to the people" (Acts 17:5-9). The rulers of the city listened to Jason and the others, were satisfied and let them go. In Greek legend he is represented as bishop of Tarsus going with St. Sosipater to Corfu evangelizing that island and dying there. Even in prison they converted seven thieves. The Syrians venerate him as a martyr thrown to the beasts. Jason is the patron of converts.

Another St. Jason, whose feast day is December 3, was beheaded with his brother St. Maurus. Their parents, Claudius, a Roman tribune, and Hilaria, who buried her sons, were caught praying at their sons' tomb and were also martyred.

"Blessed are they who suffer persecution for justice sake for theirs is the Kingdom of Heaven. Blessed are you when men reproach you and persecute you and speak falsely, say all manner of evil against you, for My sake. Rejoice and exult because your reward in heaven is great. Matt 5:10-12.

O God, Jason used the talents You gave him as an upright, prominent citizen of Salonika to aid Paul and Silas in evangelizing souls and later gave his life completely for You. Through his intercession grant that we may become like him, generous in Your service. Amen.

Jay, Jayson

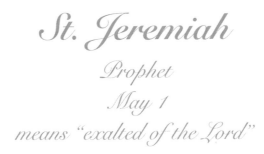

St. Jeremiah

Prophet
May 1
means "exalted of the Lord"

Jeremiah was a priest from the tribe of Benjamin. Since the time that he was in his mother's womb, Jeremiah was consecrated, that is, set apart, for God's sacred use as a prophet. He helped King Josiah reform the kingdom after the discovery of the Book of the Law in 624 BC, but once this king died, Jeremiah faced opposition from the kings that followed. He invited the people of Judah to repent and to place their trust in the Lord, yet he was scorned and accused of treason. Jeremiah was imprisoned on the grounds of blasphemy for foretelling the destruction of Jerusalem and the Babylonian captivity. He died in Egypt where he had forewarned his people not to go, but they disobediently did. Jeremiah wept over the suffering he endured both in prophesying against his nation and being rejected and persecuted by them, yet he eventually understood that God was always with him.

He was what his name indicates "Great before the Lord" and a special figure of Jesus Christ in his suffering for his people, his charity for his persecutors, and in the violent death he suffered at their hands. It was the ancient tradition of the Jews that he was stoned to death by the demand of Jews who had retired into Egypt.

In the Book of Machabees in the Old Testament the high priest, Onias, while seeing a vision of Jeremias says, "This is he that prays much for the people, and for all the holy city, Jeremias, the prophet of God." Jeremias was appearing as the special patron and guardian of Jerusalem. In the same way saints who have been chosen and devoutly honored as special patrons of individual Christians or of parishes, villages, or estates, intercede for those committed to their care.

Lord God, give me the words of consolation and truth so that I may be a beacon of light for others in the darkness of sin. Amen.

Jerry, Jeremy, Dermot

St. Jerome

Doctor of the Church
September 30
means "holy name"

St. Jerome was born in 342 in Dalmatia. His devout father took special care to educate his son both at home and then sending him to Rome. Jerome excelled in his studies, mastering Latin and Greek, and oratory. Within a short time he was a lawyer, and without falling into grave sin, Jerome began to take on the ways of the world, seeming to forget his father's formative efforts. Once on a trip with a friend, his religious spirit was awakened, encouraging him to keep company with saintly persons. He withdrew into the desert of Chalcis for four years where he tempered his body and stubborn spirit. Art often depicts Jerome with a lion because he pulled a thorn from the beast's paw and the lion befriended him for this favor. During this desert retreat he studied Hebrew. Jerome then left for Antioch to become a priest, and afterwards traveled to Palestine to join the monastery in Bethlehem. Jerome is known for his highly acclaimed work of translating the Bible into Latin, a job the Pope commissioned him to do. Today the result of this task, the Latin Vulgate, is still admired and praised. Jerome died in 420 in Bethlehem. His body now rests in Rome. St. Jerome is the patron of librarians.

Quotes of St. Jerome:
"There is no doubt that through the reading of the Sacred Scriptures the soul is set aflame in God and becomes purified of all vices."
"An importunity becomes our opportunity."
"As soon as lust assails us, let us instantly say, 'Lord, assist me; do not permit me to offend You!'"
"Go down into the abyss, you evil appetites! I will drown you lest I myself be drowned!"
"You will advance in proportion as you deny your own self."

Lord, You gave St. Jerome a great love for Holy Scripture. Let Your people feed more abundantly on Your word and find in it the source of life. Amen.

Jerry, Jeronimo, Hieronymus, Hieronyma (feminine of Jerome)

St. Joan of Arc
Martyr
May 30
means "the Lord's grace"

In 1412, Joan was born to a poor farming family in France. She herded sheep and worked on the farm with her brothers. When she was thirteen, Joan began to hear what she called "voices". In 1429, when she turned seventeen, Joan knew that it was time for her to act. The voices of three saints-St. Michael, St. Margaret, and St. Catherine of Alexandria-told her that she was to save France. She visited the Dauphin of France to tell him what God was asking of her and he granted her an army of soldiers. She dressed like a knight, carried a banner inscribed with the names "Jesus" and "Mary," and led victories for France over England. The Dauphin was crowned King Charles VII of France, but the victories of the "Maid of France" as Joan was known then, were brief. The English captured her, and King Charles VII did nothing to save France's heroine. She was imprisoned for nine months and burnt at the stake in 1431 at the young age of nineteen. While the flames consumed her, an English soldier held a cross before her eyes and she died saying, "Jesus, Jesus!" Before such a spectacle, one person said aloud, "God, have pity on us, for we have burnt a saint." St. Joan is the patron of France, soldiers, and virginity.

Dear St. Joan, grant us the courage to fight the heavenly battle for God's reign in all of mankind's heart. Through your intercession, may we bear the armor of virtue and holiness. Amen.

Jeanne, Jessica, Janette, Netty, Jenny, Joanne

Pope John Paul II and Rome

St. Peter was chosen by Jesus as the first among the apostles when Jesus said, "you are Peter and upon this rock I will build My Church." The history of the Church's Papacy in the city of Rome has an interesting background. In the year 64, at 67 years of age, Peter was crucified in the Circus of Nero at the base of the Vatican hill. Buried among the poor in a cemetery on the side of the Vatican hill overlooking the Circus of Nero, his tomb became a place of pilgrimage and veneration among early Christians. Constantine the Great, after his conversion in 315, decided to level the Vatican hill in order to erect a basilica directly over the tomb of St. Peter. In the sixteenth century, the newest basilica which replaced Constantine's was built on Peter, "the Rock." It is because of Peter's burial place in Rome that all bishops who succeed Peter as bishop of Rome are the first among the bishops of the world. Pope John Paul II succeeds St. Peter as bishop of Rome. Many Popes who served in St. Peter's stead throughout the centuries are buried near St. Peter in the crypt of the Basilica. Their burial above St. Peter's tomb is symbolic of the marriage God has wanted between Peter's successors and the city of Rome.

"Consequence, for the Rosary to become more fully a "compendium of the Gospel," it is fitting to add, following reflection on the Incarnation and the hidden life of Christ (the Joyful Mysteries) and before focusing on the sufferings of his Passion (the Sorrowful Mysteries) and the triumph of His resurrection (the Glorious Mysteries), a meditation on certain particularly significant moments in His public ministry (the Mysteries of Light). This addition of these new mysteries, without prejudice to any essential aspect of the prayer's traditional format, is meant to give it fresh life and to enkindle renewed interest in the Rosary's place within Christian spirituality as a true doorway to the depth of the heart of Christ, ocean of joy and of light, of suffering and of glory."
Taken from the Apostolic Letter, Rosarium Virginis Mariae.
Written by Pope John Paul II, October 16, 2002.

Holy Spirit, grant that all those who seek the truth recognize the primacy and divine mission bestowed on the Pope as the bishop of Rome and leader of the Catholic Church. May we all adhere to the Holy Father with loyalty, faith, love, and obedience. Amen.

John Paul, Sean Paul, Shawn Paul

St. John Mary Vianney

Confessor

August 4

means "precious gift of God" "star of the sea" (Mary)

John Mary Baptist Vianney was born to a poor family in France in 1789. Since a boy, he wanted to be a priest. John did become a priest, but because he was not very intelligent, the bishop assigned him to the small town of Ars. Then John dedicated himself to the sanctity of every soul in his parish. The townspeople became so exemplary and John so renowned for holiness that people throughout Europe went to consult him. He diverted attention from his miracles to the power of the children's prayers to St. Philomena, the beloved virgin martyr. For years, John's daily meal consisted of a few boiled potatoes. He offered other such bodily sacrifices for love of Christ and for the sake of souls. He spent sixteen to eighteen hours a day hearing confessions. He died in 1862 at the age of 73 and his body is incorrupt. St. John is the patron saint of parish priests and confessors.

Quotes of St. John Mary Vianney:

"For the Lord is there quite close to us, looking on us with kindness, smiling at us, and saying: 'So you do love Me.'"

"Prayer is to our soul what rain is to the soil. Fertilize the soil ever so richly, it will remain barren unless fed by frequent rains."

"The more we pray, the more we wish to pray---the soul---loses itself in the sweetness of conversing with God."

"The pure soul is a beautiful rose, and the Three Divine Persons descend from Heaven to inhale its fragrance."

Lord, with the help of St. John Mary Vianney may we grow in our appreciation for our parish priests and for the sacrament of confession so that we will be touched by Your graces. Amen.

St. Joseph
Husband of Our Lady and Foster Father of Jesus
March 19
means "he shall add"

St. Joseph, described as "a just man," was chosen by God to be the Blessed Mother's protector and Jesus' foster-father. He is the patron of the Universal Church since he was the head of the Holy Family. He was humble, upright, and obedient. Joseph was present throughout Jesus' life: his birth, the presentation of the Christ child in the Temple, the plight into Egypt, the finding of Child in the Temple, and His years before His public ministry. Jesus not only learned carpentry from His father Joseph, but he learned His manner of speaking and acting, as most boys do. Tradition holds that St. Joseph died with the Virgin Mary and Jesus at his side. That is why we pray to him for a happy death. St. Joseph is also the patron of husbands, fathers, Belgium, Canada, home real estate, and the Universal Church. More recently, he has been prayed to for the end of Communism.

Many saints speak of his very special intercession with the God who often slept upon the pure and gentle heart of Joseph. St. Theresa of Avila, Blessed Andre Bessette, St. Frances Cabrini, and Solanius Casey are among the many saints who have obtained blessings through the intercession of St. Joseph. Theresa of Avila is called "the patron saint for the devotion to St. Joseph."

St. Joseph, father and guardian of virgins, into whose faithful care were entrusted innocence itself, Christ Jesus, and Mary the Virgin of Virgins, I pray and beseech thee through Jesus and Mary, those pledges so dear to thee, to preserve me from all uncleanness and to grant that my mind may be untainted, my heart pure and my body chaste; help me always to serve Jesus and Mary in perfect chastity. Amen.

Almighty God, You entrusted to the faithful care of Joseph the beginnings of the mysteries of salvation. Through his intercession may Your Church always be faithful in her service so that Your designs will be fulfilled. Amen.

Joe, Jo, Josie, Jody, Josephine, Josepha, Giussepi, Joel, Joetta

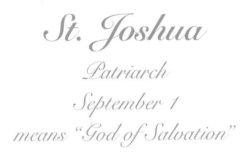

St. Joshua

Patriarch

September 1

means "God of Salvation"

As Moses' lieutenant, Joshua led the Israelite army into battle against Amalek. He also accompanied Moses to Mount Sinai where Moses received the Ten Commandments from God. Throughout Moses' life, Joshua was a faithful and honest companion. God blessed Joshua's fidelity by making him lead Israel into the Promised Land after Moses died. God helped Joshua and the Israelites conquer the city of Jericho as well as the cities that followed. Joshua continually inspired the Israelites to be faithful to their covenant with God.

"And Israel served the Lord all the days of Joshua and of the ancients that lived a long time after Joshua and that had known all the works of the Lord which he had done in Israel. - Joshua that son of Nun, the servant of the Lord died, being a hundred and ten years old; - and they buried him on the north side of Mount Gaas." Joshua 24:29-30, 31

Quotes of St. Joshua:
"As for me and my house, we will serve the Lord." Joshua 24:15
"Be ye satisfied: for tomorrow the Lord will do wonders among you." Joshua 3:5

St. Joshua, as you pleased God with your fidelity, teach me to never forsake my Lord and to willingly pay the cost of this friendship. Amen.

Josh, Josua, Josue

St. Juan Diego

Visionary
December 9

Juan Diego was 51 years old when he, his wife, and his uncle were baptized in 1525. He took the Christian names Juan Diego (John James). It was on the Spanish feast of the Immaculate Conception December 9, 1531 on his way to Mass that he heard music from Mount Tepeyac and saw a beautiful woman standing before a bright cloud. She asked him to tell the bishop to build a church on the mount. Having explained this to the bishop, the bishop told Juan that he would need to bring him proof. On December 12, Mary told Juan to gather some roses that were blooming on the hillside. Mary arranged the roses and Juan carried them in his tilma to the bishop. When Juan opened the tilma, the roses fell to the floor unveiling the miraculous image of Our Lady of Guadalupe. The chapel was built and Juan became the guardian of the heavenly treasure and evangelized millions of Aztecs for they could see represented in the tilma the woman who crushes the stone serpent and overcomes the mother-goddess with her purity of faith. Juan died in 1548 and was canonized July 31, 2002. He is the patron of the lay ministry.

"Happy Juan Diego, true and faithful man! We entrust to you our lay brothers and sisters so that, feeling the call to holiness, they may imbue every area of social life with the spirit of the Gospel. Bless families, strengthen spouses in their marriage, sustain the efforts of parents to give their children a Christian upbringing. Look with favor upon the pain of those who are suffering in body or in spirit, on those afflicted by poverty, loneliness, marginalization or ignorance. May all people, civic leaders, and ordinary citizens, always act in accordance with the demands of justice and with respect for the dignity of each person, so that in this way peace may be reinforced."
End of Beatification Sermon of Pope John Paul II

Quote of Our Lady to Juan Diego:
"Listen and keep in your heart that there is nothing for you to fear. Let neither your face nor your heart be worried. Am I not here, I who am your mother? Are you not in the fold of my mantle, in the crossing of my arms? Is there anything else you need?"

Beloved Juan Diego, "the talking eagle"! Show us the way that leads to the "Dark Virgin" of Tepeyac, that she may receive us in the depth of her heart, for she is the loving, compassionate mother who guides us to the true God. Amen

St. Judith

Old Testament Heroine
September 14
means "praised"

Judith was a young, beautiful widow who saved her people, the Israelites, from Nabuchadnezer, the Assyrian King. Nebuchadnezer wanted to punish all other nations that did not acknowledge his greatness and power. He told the general of his armies, Holofernes, "go out against all the kingdoms of the west, and against them especially that despised my commandment." Holofernes was relentless and blood thirsty in executing this order. The Israelites feared attack, but one wise woman, respected for her fortitude, piety, and stunning beauty prayed to God on behalf of her doubting Israelites. With preparation that consisted of prayer, fasting, and penance, Judith bravely carried out God's plan for her to defeat Holofernes. He who had slaughtered many strong nations would lose his life by a woman's hand. One night of drunkenness found him asleep in his tent when Judith used his own sword to cut off his head. Thus, Judith saved her people from the wrath of the Assyrians by her heroic cunning.

Judith is a prototype of the Virgin Mary in the saving of her people with great fortitude and love.

St. Jutta or Judith was inspired by St. Elizabeth of Hungary. A native of the same area, she was an exemplary widow who raised her children alone after her husband died on a Holy Land pilgrimage. Her children all became religious, so she was free to be a recluse. She wished to be most humble and forgotten, gave all to the poor, becoming a beggar, herself caring for other destitute and sick people. She received wonderful graces, revelations, and an infused understanding of Scripture. She said three things could bring one near to God - painful illness, foreign exile and poverty for God's sake. Jutta is the patroness of Prussia. She died of a fever in 1260.

Almighty Father, these saints, both widows, served You in Your people in an outstanding way. Help us to imitate their prayerfulness, courage and charity. Amen.

Judy, Jutta, Yvette

St. Kenneth

Abbot

October 11

means "leader"

Kenneth or Canice, the son of an Irish bard, went over to Wales, became a monk, and was ordained when he was a young man. He traveled, preached, founded monasteries, and evangelized Scotland with St. Columba. When in danger at sea, St. Columba said to his companions, "Don't be afraid! God will listen to Kenneth who is running to the church with one shoe on to pray for us." Meanwhile, back in Ireland, Kenneth was miraculously made aware of his friend's peril and jumped up from a meal to go to pray in the church. One amazing miracle was wrought by Kenneth when a petty chieftain raised his hand with a sword to kill the monks accompanying Kenneth. He paralyzed the chieftain's hand and saved the day. A legend speaks of Kenneth's "O" which he left unfinished while doing calligraphy with black ink when the bell rang in the monastery calling him to prayer. When he returned to his unfinished work, he realized that his obedience to the life in the monastery was rewarded with an "O" written in gold calligraphy by his angel. St. Kenneth is the patron of Kilkenny, Ireland.

"For as by one man's disobedience many were made sinners, so by one man's obedience may all be made righteous." Rom 5:19

Dear St. Kenneth, from the rich roster of the saints you come forth as a missionary friend of St. Columba whose comradery with you evoked a great sense of humor. Through your intercession grant us to see the lighter side of life in all our hardships, so we can travel joyously toward heaven, there to praise God forever with you. Amen.

Canice, Kenny, Ken, Kendra

St. Kevin

Abbot

June 3

means "comely"

St. Kevin was born of royal descent in Leinster, Ireland at the Fort of the White Fountain. He was baptized by St. Cronan, and from the age of 7 was educated and reared by monks at his parents' request. After his ordination, an angel led him to live in solitude for seven years in upper Glendalough, in the wild and beautiful Valley of the Two Lakes. While existing under such austerity, "the branches and leaves of the trees sometimes sang sweet songs to him, and heavenly music alleviated the severity of his life." Legend has it that a cattle farmer named Dima discovered Kevin in a cave and urged him to leave his solitude. He did, and created a settlement for the disciples who came to him, among whom was St. Owen, another popular name saint. Legend states that "a kindly otter brought a salmon everyday to supply them with nourishment." Kevin moved his community to Glendalough. Then Kevin made a pilgrimage to Rome to beg a blessing upon him and his disciples. An old Irish saying states that "because of the holy relics and mould which he brought back, no single saint in Erin ever obtained more from God than Kevin, save Patrick only."

It is passed down that the holy abbot, an intimate friend of St. Kieran, went to visit him on his deathbed. Kieran was either dead or unconscious already, but when St. Kevin arrived, he returned to life or consciousness long enough to hold holy conversation with Kevin before death. Legend tells us that St. Kevin died in Glendalough at the age of 120, about the year 618. Ireland still celebrates his feast day on June 3. He is the patron of longevity.

Holy Spirit, as you directed St. Kevin to enjoy Your company during his life as a hermit, may I look for a moment of solitude daily so I can listen to You directing my heart. Amen.

Kevina

St. Leo the Great

Pope and Doctor of the Church
November 10

means "lion"

Leo's family was from Tuscany. Leo received a good education and served as a deacon under Pope St. Celestine I and then Sixtus III. He showed his talents as a statesman and diplomat long before his papal consecration on September 29, 440. Pope Leo had to be strong to lead the young Church through the rough times of heresies, barbarian attacks, and the decline of the Roman Empire. Among the problems he had to address were the barbarian invasions in Rome. In 452, Pope Leo met Attila the Hun outside of Rome, and with great diplomatic skill, he persuaded the leader of the Huns not to enter Rome. In 455, he was not so successful in his dealings with Genseric, leader of the Vandals. Genseric still plundered Rome, but promised Pope Leo that he would kill no one. Thus, Pope Leo saved Rome on two occasions.

Contending with the "Robber Synod" of 450 AD, Leo called the Council of Chalcedon in 451 which declared the previous synod null and void, and pronounced the true doctrine regarding Jesus' two-fold nature (human and divine). His definition, called the "Tome of Leo," roused the assembly of bishops to unanimously declare "Peter has spoken by Leo!" Leo died November 10, 461 and his relics remain in St. Peter's basilica. He is the patron of choirs.

Quote of St. Leo:
"'Precious in the eyes of the Lord is the death of his faithful ones,' and no kind of cruelty can destroy a religion that is founded upon the mystery of the Cross of Christ. Persecutions do not diminish the Church, indeed, they cause it to develop. The martyrs are a gift of God, an aid to our weakness, and example of virtue and support to our faith."

Loving Father, You established Your Church on the solid rock of St. Peter. Grant that she may persevere through the intercession of St. Leo. Amen.

Leon, Lee, Leona, Lionel

St. Linda (Ermelinda)

Queen and Abbess

February 13

means "world serpent"

Saints born of saints, nurtured and educated by saints and associating again with other saints-such was England in the 7th and 8th centuries, and it reads like a story book!

One of these saints was Ermelinda, daughter of St. Sexburga. Her aunt was St. Audrey (Etheldreda). St. Chad, bishop of Litchfield, instructed and baptized this family. St. Ermelinda was the mother of the beautiful and talented virgin, St. Wereburga and three sons, one of whom was Coenrad, who became a monk in Rome.

Sexburga, Audrey, and Ermelinda were English queens and later in quick succession abbesses at the monastery built by Audrey at Ely.

Wereburga took her vows as a nun at Chester and there a charming little legend is spun around the wonderful miracles of St. Wereburga. The Archbishop of Canterbury, St. Dunstan, started to weep while praying at the dedication of the church she and her nuns had invited him to officiate at. When asked why the tears, he replied that it was because she was soon to leave this earth. She was only in her early twenties when she died, but her soul was already perfected for eternity.

Dear God, through Your Son, Jesus and His dear parents, Mary and Joseph, You set the example for many holy families through the centuries. Grant us a great flourishing of holiness in society again through the intercession of these many, many saints. Amen.

Erma, Linda, Melinda, Erminilda

St. Louis IX

King of France
August 25
means "bold warrior"

Louis became the King of France at twelve years of age, and he bore in mind his mother's wish that she would rather see her son die than commit a mortal sin. His mother was Blessed Blanche. At the age of fourteen he combated the Albigensian heresy. Besides caring for matters of his temporal kingdom, Louis made time each day to hear two Masses and recite the Divine Office. In 1248, against the advice of his court, he undertook the seventh crusade to recapture the Holy Land from the Turks. Louis paid the ransom of Christian slaves and had some success, but he himself was captured. His life was threatened at sword point more than once, but he never denied his faith. He returned to France after his people ransomed him. During the sixteen years that Louis reigned, France flourished like never before. He prepared to return to the Holy Land a second time. In August of 1270, Louis and his army landed in Tunis, Egypt, and though he achieved victory, he caught a malignant fever. He received Viaticum kneeling at the side of his camp bed and died as honorably as he had lived. He is the patron of tertiaries and traders (especially of horses), barbers, and printers. In the picture, Louis is carrying the crown of thorns to Le Chapele, which he had designed, to enshrine it.

Quote of St. Louis IX:
"In prosperity, give thanks to God with humility and fear lest by pride you abuse God's benefits and so offend him."

Heavenly Father, although King Louis was committed to the cares of his kingdom in France, he never neglected his service to Your Heavenly Kingdom. Through his intercession, may Your faithful always place their first and greatest interest in Your Divine Kingdom. Amen.

Louie, Lewis, Lou, Louise, Lois

St. Madeleine Sophie Barat

Virgin and Foundress

May 25

means "from Magdala" Sophie means "wisdom"

Madeleine was born December 12, 1779 in France. Her older brother Louis was her godfather and her future teacher. When he returned home after becoming a deacon, he found his ten-year-old sister so bright and beaming with potential that he knew God had a special mission in store for her. He made it his personal duty to educate and form her as well as possible by demanding only the best from her in every aspect. After the French Revolution there was a need to rebuild the Catholic schools. A priest named Fr. Varin was interested in finding a strong woman to found a new congregation of religious sisters who would make their primary duty the education of youth. Fr. Varin discovered the qualities, due to Louis' careful formation, in Madeleine. She devoted herself to the foundation of this new order called the Society of the Sacred Heart. However, as often happens with founders, when she was away establishing new houses, a new chaplain and one of her local superiors made changes without Mother Barat's consultation. It came to the point where the new order's charism and even its name were about to be altered, but with Fr. Varin's help things were set straight. Pope Leo XII approved the Society of the Sacred Heart in 1826. Mother Barat remained superior general for sixty-three years until she died on the feast of the Ascension, May 25, 1865.

Quotes of St. Madeleine Sophie Barat:
"We must suffer in order to go to God. We forget this truth far too often."
"You say you are weak? Have you fathomed the strength of God?"

Lord Jesus Christ, after the model of Your Sacred Heart, You wonderfully graced St. Madeleine Sophie with humility and love. Make us cling to Your most Sacred Heart and find our joy in becoming Your companions. Amen.

Madelyn, Maddy, Lena, Sophia, Sonia, Sonya

St. Mary Magdalen

Apostle
July 22
Mary means "lady" Magdalen means "from Magdala"

Mary came from Magdala in Galilee. Before she met Jesus she lived a scandalous life. It is thought that Jesus cast seven demons from her, and touched by His pure love and grace, she converted her life-style and became one of Jesus' closest friends and companions. Jesus enjoyed spending time at her home in Bethany with her brother Lazarus and her sister Martha. Simon the Pharisee once judged Mary for her lavish love for Jesus, and in response to Simon's thoughts, Jesus told Mary that her many sins were forgiven because her love was so great. Mary's love was tested and proven as she stood at the foot of Jesus' cross and traveled to His tomb early Easter morning, only to be rewarded with meeting the risen Lord. After Pentecost, tradition has it that she went into the desert and lived as a hermitess. She died about the year 77 AD. The forehead of her skull still bears the immortality of His risen touch of two fingertips. The skin there remains incorrupt!

Easter Sequence:
"O Mary what did your wondering eyes adore?
I saw the tomb of One who dies no more!
The glorious risen Lord was shown to me.
The napkin, linen cloths there lying.
I heard the angels testifying.
Yes, Christ is risen and you shall see Your Hope and mine in Galilee!"

Lord Jesus, left to ourselves we fall into grave sin. Through St. Mary Magdalen's intercession shower upon those who are hardened in their sins the grace of conversion and love for purity and virtue. Amen.

Magdalene, Lena, Maud

St. Maximilian Kolbe

Martyr

August 14

means "the great Emil"

(from the martyr St. Emil-means "calm" ◆ *May 28)*

Maximilian Kolbe was born in Poland on January 7, 1894. The Virgin Mary appeared to him when he was a child and she offered him two crowns: one for purity and one for martyrdom; Maximilian chose both. He joined the Friars Minor Conventional (the Franciscans). After his ordination in Rome in 1918, Maximilian returned to Poland and founded a community of Franciscans that would spread worldwide devotion to Mary. He founded a magazine called "Knight of the Immaculate" to spread her devotion. Maximilian traveled to Japan and India to achieve his spiritual goal: "the conquest of the whole world and every living soul for the Sacred Heart of Jesus through His Immaculate Mother." Due to poor health, Maximilian returned to Poland and was arrested in 1941 by the Nazis. He died in the Auschwitz concentration camp on August 14, 1941 when he offered his life in place of another prisoner who was the father of a family. He is the patron of drug addicts.

Quotes of St. Maximilian Kolbe:

"Every man and woman in this world has been assigned a mission by God. In fact ever since God created the universe, He arranged the first causes in such a way that the unbroken chain of their effects should create the most favorable conditions and circumstances for each person to fulfill the mission that God has assigned him."

"Sanctity is not a luxury, but a simple duty."

Dear St. Maximilian, increase my love for my Blessed Mother and for my neighbor so that I defend them with my own life, if needs be. Amen.

Max, Maxine, Emil

St. Michael

Archangel

September 29

means "who is like unto God?"

God created many and varied angels, all with specific tasks, divine intelligence, and free will to love and serve Him. According to St. John's book of Revelation, there was a great battle in heaven among the angels. One of the greater angels named Lucifer became proud because he was so beautifully made, and gathered a band of disobedient angels around him, rallying, "I will not serve God!" Another powerful angel cried out with love for God, "Mi-cha-el: Who is like God?" He and the other angels defeated Lucifer and the rebellious angels and cast them into hell. As a reward for his great love and obedience, God made the Archangel Michael prince of the angelic army. That is why he is the leader of God's people and the protector of the Catholic Church. Around May 8, 492 A.D. he appeared in a large cave in Mount Garganus in Italy and manifested his desire that the spot be consecrated in his honor. A healing spring trickles there beside the crypt altar. Mount St. Michael on the French coast is another place of healing up high in a beautiful Benedictine cliff shrine with a fantastic view indeed worthy of the this great prince who has become known from earliest times as one of God's great healers. His statue now stands on Hadrian's tomb across the bridge of Bernini's Angels over the Tiber, because healing of the plague ravaging Rome emanated from Michael's presence there in the reign of St. Gregory the Great. Now the tomb is called the Castle of St. Angels. St. Michael is the patron of policemen and grocers. He is also the patron of Germany.

St. Michael, the Archangel, defend us in battle; be our safeguard against the wickedness and snares of the devil. May God rebuke him, we humbly pray, and do thou, O Prince of the Heavenly Host, by the power of God, cast into hell Satan and all the other evil spirits who roam about the world seeking the ruin of souls. Amen.

Mitchell, Mike, Mikhail, Mickey, Michaeline, Shelley, Michaela, Michelle

Our Lady of Fatima
October 13

In 1917, the Mother of God appeared at Fatima in Portugal. There she invited all souls to find refuge in her Immaculate Heart saying, "Jesus wants to establish in the world devotion to my Immaculate Heart." The Blessed Mother's Immaculate Heart serves as the model of perfect love toward God and neighbor and invites us to make reparation for sins and to receive the sacraments frequently and worthily. Our Lady at Fatima said that her Immaculate Heart will triumph through the following means: daily recitation of the rosary, sacrifices for the conversion of sinner and the consecration of Russia. Devotion to the Immaculate Heart is intimately related to the Sacred Heart of Jesus.

Hymn of Our Lady of Fatima

*Dear Lady of Fatima, we come on
bended knee to beg your intercession
for peace and unity.*

*Dear Mary, won't you show us the
right and shining way. We pledge our
love and offer you, a rosary each day.*

*You promised at Fatima each time
that your appeared, to help us if
we pray to you to banish war and fear.*

*Dear Lady on first Saturdays we ask
your guiding hand, for grace and guidance
here on earth and protection for our land.*

"Dear Mother, may we through your Rosary ADD purity to the world, SUBTRACT evil from our lives, MULTIPLY good works for your Son, and DIVIDE your gifts and share them with others."

My Queen! My Mother! I give you all of myself, and to show my devotion to you, I consecrate to you my eyes, my ears, my mouth, my entire self. Wherefore, O loving Mother, as I am your own, keep me and defend me as your property and possession. Amen.

Fatima

St. Peregrine

Confessor

May 1

means "stranger, traveler"

Peregrine was born in Italy in 1260 to a financially comfortable family. As a young man, Peregrine belonged to an anti-papal party, and during an uprising, he struck St. Philip Benizi who was sent by the pope to be a mediator. St. Philip reacted by turning the other cheek, upon which Peregrine was converted. He turned to the Blessed Virgin Mary, spending hours praying before her image in the cathedral. She appeared and advised him to "Go to Siena. There you will find the devout men who call themselves my servants. Attach yourself to them." He joined the Servites and became a model priest. He lived by the principle of never resting when it comes to exercising virtue. He carefully observed solitude and silence, and he "was never known to sit down in thirty years." He was most fervent in celebrating the sacraments and eloquent in preaching.

Peregrine suffered cancer in his foot. The night before the operation that would amputate his foot, he fell into a deep slumber. When he woke his cancer had been healed. He died at eighty years of age. St. Peregrine is the patron of cancer patients and those with hernias or skin diseases.

Four hundred years after burial, the body of "The Cancer Saint" was found to be incorrupt.

Prayer for Cancer Patients

St. Pergrine, lest I lose confidence I beg your kind intercession. Plead with Mary, the Mother of Sorrow, whom you loved so tenderly and in union with whom you have suffered the pain of cancer, that she may help me with her all powerful prayers and consolation. Obtain for me the strength to accept my trials from the loving hand of God with patience and resignation. May suffering lead me to a better life and enable me to atone for my own sins and the sins of the world. St. Peregrine, help me to imitate you in bearing whatever cross God may permit to come to me, uniting myself with Jesus crucified and the Mother of Sorrows. I offer my sufferings to God with all the love of my heart, for his glory and the salvation of souls especially my own. Amen.

Perry

St. Philip

Apostle and Martyr

May 11

means "lover of horses"

In St. John's Gospel, it says that Jesus "found Philip" and said, "Follow me." Philip went at once to find his friend Nathaniel and said, "We have found him of whom Moses in the law and the prophets did write." Nathaniel answered, "Can anything good come from Nazareth?" But Philip patiently appealed, "Come and see." Already he showed missionary zeal with a sober discretion. At the feeding of the 5,000 Jesus said to Philip, "Where shall we buy bread that these may eat?" Philip replied, "Two hundred penny worth of bread is not sufficient that everyone may take a little." He took his Divine Master literally! Later on, earnest and devoted, Philip asked Jesus, "Lord, show us the Father, and it is enough for us." Jesus replied, "Have I been so long a time with you; and have you not known me? Philip, he who sees me, sees the Father."

At Pentecost, Philip's spiritual insight was empowered and he was filled with the Holy Spirit. He evangelized mainly in Phrygia and at Hierpolis, and was buried there with two of his three daughters, both virgins who lived to be very old. These daughters told of a dead man being raised to life by Philip. Clement of Alexandria says he suffered up side-down crucifixion under Emperor Domitian.

Quote of St. Philip Neri:
"Never trust to yourself either on the ground of experience or length of time, or age, or sickness; but always fly from every occasion of danger as long as you have strength to raise your eyelids." (From the Chapter entitled "Lean on God")

O devoted Apostle, Philip, plead for us to Jesus for the grace to be zealous in bringing others to the Faith that we may all see the Father now in Jesus and then forever face to face. Amen.

Phil, Flip, Filipe, Phyllis

St. Philomena

Virgin and Martyr

August 11

means "daughter of light"

Sometimes in a flower garden a different little bud pushes through the soil later in the season and surprises the gardener with a special bloom, a delightful volunteer. So it was with Philomena, a Greek princess and martyr from back in Emperor Diocletian's time, who came to light in 1802 as a saint in the Church from the catacombs, jolting us back to God and His unique surprises of love. Even though there is no solid proof of the existence of this saint, intercession to her has brought about many wonders and even miracles, especially for students and parents wanting babies. The Cure of Ars "blamed" her for his miracles. They worked as a team even filling an empty storeroom with grain for the orphanage. The foundress of the Propagation of the Faith, Venerable Pauline Jaricot, was brought back to life at death's door through St. Philomena's intercession. Philomena's bones are enshrined at Magnano, Italy, and the most beautiful outdoor shrine containing a white carrara marble statue is just a few miles above Wisconsin Dells near a small village church.

St. Philomena, happy virgin, adorned with all the charm of innocence, and beautified, besides, with the purple of martyrdom, obtain for us the grace to know how to suffer all and to sacrifice all in order to be faithful to God until death and possess Him eternally in Paradise. Amen.

St. Philomena, spouse of Christ, who resisted the allurements of this world set before you by Diocletian who lusted for you, intercede for all who need spiritual strength in this dark world. Amen.

Philomene, Penny

St. Pio of Pietrelcina

Pastor

September 23

means "dutiful, filial, pious"

In the humble countryside of Pietrelcina, Italy on May 25, 1887 a baby was born who would be a consolation and bring great healing, spiritual and physical, to the Church of the 20th century. He was Padre Pio, a Capuchin Franciscan priest and teacher of seminarians. The morning of Friday, September 20, 1918, praying before the crucifix in the choir of the old church, he received the gift of the stigmata, which did not heal, but bled for half a century. The gifts of prophecy, healing, bilocation, and reading souls gave him great popularity for the benefit of humanity, but he was also persecuted as a fraud and severely confined for a time. He offered himself as a victim for sinners and for the souls in Purgatory. During his life, he founded prayer groups and a modern hospital, to which he gave the name "Home for the Relief of Suffering." He also defended the Pope's Humanae Vitae prohibiting birth control. On September 23, 1968 he died and was canonized on June 16, 2002.

Padre Pio's Thoughts for the Relief of Suffering

"A Man who transcending himself, bends over the wounds of his less fortunate brother, raises to the Lord the most beautiful, the most noble prayer, made of sacrifice and love. I know that all of you are suffering. Take courage! The trust in our Mother is the sure guarantee that she will stretch out her hand to comfort us."

"In every suffering there is Jesus who suffers! In every poor man there is Jesus who is wretched! In every poor sick person there is twice Jesus, who is suffering and wretched! Let us always be aware of the needs of our brother if we want the Lord Our God to bless us and bless our families."

O God, may St. Pio, to whom You donated the grace to participate in a wonderful way in the Passion of Your Son, concede to us, through his intercession, to conform ourselves to the death of Jesus, to attain then to the glory of the Resurrection. We ask this through Christ our Lord. Amen.

Pious, Pia, Piedad

St. Rachel

Jacob met Rachel when he went to work for his uncle Laban. He fell in love with her immediately and requested her hand from his uncle. His uncle, however, required that Jacob work seven years on his farm before he would be able to marry Rachel. This he agreed to do, but when the term was up his uncle Laban deceived him. Jacob ended up marrying Rachel's sister, Lia. When Jacob discovered his uncle's trick he was angry. Laban told him that he would have to work on the farm seven more years to have Rachel as his wife also, even though Jacob only wanted one wife, and that wife to be Rachel. Jacob agreed and finally married her after fourteen years of waiting. At first she was barren, while Jacob had many children with her sister Lia. At last Rachel conceived a son named Joseph who would save the nation. Rachel died giving birth to Benjamin, her second son. She is the patron of mothers who lose or grieve for aborted children because her future descendents, the Holy Innocents from the surrounding area of Bethlehem, were the victims of Herod's jealousy and slaughtered, as the children of the womb are today. The building shown on Rachel's holy card is her tomb in Bethlehem.

"A voice was heard on high of lamentation, of mourning, and weeping, of Rachel weeping for her children, and refusing to be comforted for them, because they are not."
Jeremiah Chapter 13 Verse 15

"Thus saith the Lord: Let thy voice cease from weeping, and thy eyes from the tears, for there is a reward for the work, saith the Lord; and they shall return out of the land of the enemy." Verse 16

"Jesus, Mary, Joseph I love you very much. I beg You to spare the life of the unborn child that I have spiritually adopted from the danger of abortion. Amen. Prayer for pro-life suggested by Archbishop Fulton J. Sheen to be said every day with faith in God's love.

Grant, O God, that children will be loved and treasured as gifts from You. Amen.

Rachelle, Rachael, Shelley, Raquel

St. Raymond of Penafort

Confessor

January 23

means "wise protector"

Raymond was born in Spain in 1175. An excellent student, Raymond progressed so rapidly in school that by the age of twenty he was a philosophy teacher at Barcelona. He went on to study civil and canon law, and these professions he dispensed freely and disinterestedly to serve the community. Raymond became a Dominican when he was forty-seven years old. Although he was offered prestigious positions in the Church, he turned these down or held them only for a minimum of time so that he could return to the solitude of the monastery. He devoted much of his time and talent to defending the Church from the Moors in Europe, especially in Spain. One story is told of how Raymond accompanied King James of Aragon to the island of Majorca. When the king was behaving immorally, Raymond wished to return to Spain. Under penalty of death, the king forbade anyone to help Raymond leave the island. Undeterred, Raymond said, "An earthly king withholds the means of flight, but the King of Heaven will supply them." With that, he walked to the sea, spread his cloak over the water, tied up one part of it to his staff to act as a sail, waved the sign of the cross over his vessel before boarding it, and swiftly sailed back to Spain. Raymond died January 6, 1275 at the age of 100. He is the patron of canonists and sail fabricators. Another great saint, Raymond Nonnatus, is the patron of expectant mothers, the falsely accused, and obstetricians.

Collect from his Mass

"O God Thou didst elect blessed Raymond to be an imminent minister of the sacrament of Penance, and didst miraculously guide him through the waves of the sea. Grant that through his intercession, we may bring forth worth fruits of penance, and reach the haven of eternal life. Through Our Lord Jesus Christ, who lives with You together with the Holy Spirit forever and ever." Amen.

O God, You who granted wisdom and apostolic zeal for souls to St. Raymond, give to Your people an ardent desire to see Your Church defended and flourish within our countries. Amen.

Ramon, Ramona, Rayette, Ray, Ray Ann

St. Rebecca

Matriarch of the Old Testament
means "charmer, ensnarer"

Abraham sent his servant to seek a wife for Isaac his son. The servant spotted Rebecca, "an exceedingly comely maid, and a most beautiful virgin." She and her family agreed to the arrangement, and Rebecca returned to Isaac. Isaac loved her tenderly. She was barren for twenty years until she pleaded with God who granted her twins. God said of the children in her womb, "Two nations are in thy womb, and two peoples shall be divided out of thy womb, and one people shall overcome the other, and the elder shall serve the younger." Esau was born first, followed by Jacob. Isaac favored Esau, and Rebecca favored Jacob. Esau sold his birthright to Jacob, so when their father lay dying, Rebecca contrived a plan so that Jacob instead of Esau would receive his father's blessing which was entitled to the first-born son. Rebecca, aware of the vengeance Esau would have on his brother, counseled Jacob to flee to his uncle's house. In this way, Rebecca secured God's will that Jacob be the next leader of His people.

Two more saints are recorded by the name of Rebecca. One is especially notable as the mother of five saints, Agatho, Ammon, Ammonius, Peter and John. This valiant Rebecca was martyred in ancient Shadra. Rebecca's Feast Day is November 4th.

Parents Prayer for Their Children

O God the Father of mankind You have given me my children and committed them to my charge to bring them up for You, and to prepare them for eternal life; help me with Your heavenly grace, that I may be able to fulfill this most sacred duty and stewardship. Teach me both what to give and what to withhold; when to reprove and when to forbear; make me to be gentle, yet firm; considerate and watchful; and deliver me equally from the weakness of indulgence, and the excess of severity; and grant that both by word and example, I may be careful to lead them in the ways of wisdom and true piety, so that at last I may, with them be admitted to the unspeakable joys of our true home in heaven in the company of the blessed Angels and Saints. Amen.

Heavenly Father, grant wisdom and prudence to all mothers so that they may always desire Your will for their children's lives. Amen.

Reba, Becky, Becca

St. Richard of Wyche

Bishop
April 3
means "powerful"

St. Richard was born in 1197. His parents died prematurely and left their wealthy estate to a negligent hand who allowed it to fall into ruin. Richard recuperated the family fortune, gave it to his older brother Robert, and left penniless to study at Oxford University. Although two arrangements had been made for him to marry, Richard felt a deeper call to celibacy. He was ordained a priest in 1243. In 1244, during the time of the lay investiture abuse, King Henry III appointed an unworthy man to succeed the previous bishop of Chichester. The Archbishop refused this candidate and nominated Richard, then chancellor. In retaliation, Henry refused Richard all rightful temporalities and privileges due to his office as bishop. Then, Henry increased his disapproval of Richard, and forbade any Englander to show him hospitality, to the extent that the Chichester palace gates were closed to him. Thus treated, Richard worked as a missionary bishop, traveling by foot or by beast to visit his flock. Once Henry died, Richard's rights were reinstated. Richard was renowned for his stern stance on abuses within and outside of the Church and for his boundless charity. When his steward told him that his alms were surpassing his income, he encouraged his steward to sell his gold and silver dishes, adding, "There is my horse too...sell him also, and bring me the money for the poor." He died of a fever in 1253 at a house for poor priests and pilgrims.

There is also a Saint King Richard of the 8th century. He was the father of Saints Willibald, Wunibald, and Walburga.

Quotes of St. Richard:
"God is faithful, and if we serve Him faithfully, He will provide for your needs."
"Satisfaction consists in the cutting off of the cause of sin. Thus, fasting is the proper antidote to lust; prayer to pride, to envy, anger, and sloth; alms to covetousness."

Dear Jesus, despite the resistance I may suffer in living out my commitments in my state in life, help me to be a courageous example of a Catholic in today's world as was St. Richard. Amen.

Dick, Rick, Ricardo, Reichard

St. Robert Bellarmine

Archbishop and Doctor of the Church
May 13
means "bright in fame"

So devout was Robert as a Jesuit college student that the rector described him as "the best of our school and not far from the Kingdom of Heaven." But that was only the beginning. Robert knew Virgil by heart, was poetic, played violin, and could hold his own in debates. Ill health was his "flaw" and he was small in stature, so much so that he used a stool at the pulpit. He was ordained a Jesuit priest under the great St. Francis Borgia. He also learned Greek and Hebrew, and was a brilliant professor at Louvain, but ill health brought him back to Italy; St. Charles desired to have him in Milan, but instead he was appointed to the chair of controversial theology at the Roman College, lecturing and writing "the most complete defense of the Catholic teaching yet published", in the historian Hefele's estimation.

He was at the deathbed of St. Aloysius Gonzaga to whom he was deeply attached. He wrote two catechisms still used in Italy. Pope Clement, who named Robert a Cardinal, stated that "He had not his equal for learning." He lived on bread and garlic - the food of the poor and even used the wall hangings to clothe the poor. Then as a simple archbishop he won the love of all classes. But Rome could not abide long without his genius and he held many prominent positions there. He was a friend to Galileo but gently advised him against putting forward theories not yet proven unless as a hypothesis. He died at 79 on September 17, the feast day he set for the Stigmata of St. Francis. In 1931 he was declared a Doctor of the Church.

O God, who did fill St. Robert with wondrous learning and virtue, that he might break the snares of error and defend the Apostolic See; grant us by his merits and intercession, that we may grow in the love of Truth and that the hearts of those in error may return to the unity of the Church. Amen.

Rupert, Robin, Bob, Robby, Dobbin, Roberta

St. Sara

Abraham's Wife
August 19
means "princess"

This loyal woman was so beautiful that twice other men tried to take her from Abraham, her husband. When Abraham was ninety-nine years old, God promised him that he would be the father of many nations. Abraham loved the Lord dearly, but he could not understand how this could be since his wife Sara had bore him no children and was already ninety years old. Sara was barren, and this was a tremendous burden that grieved her. One day three angels who appeared as men stopped at Abraham's tent, and they told him that when they returned the following year Sara would have a son. When she overheard them say this, she laughed and said to herself, "Shall I who am an old woman bear a child indeed?" As with all of God's promises, Sara did conceive and bear a son, naming him Isaac as God had asked. From Isaac's offspring, God also fulfilled His promise to Abraham that his descendants would be as numerous as the stars in the sky. Sara died when she was one hundred and twenty-seven years old, and Abraham buried his faithful wife in Canaan.

Prayer from the Nuptial Mass

True and chaste may she wed in Christ and may she ever follow the pattern of holy women; and may she be dear to her husband like Rachel; wise like Rebecca; long-lived and faithful like Sara. May the author of deceit work none of his evil deeds in her. May she ever be knit to the faith and to the commandments. May she be true to one husband and fly from forbidden approaches. May she fortify her weakness by strong discipline? May she be grave in demeanor and honored for her modesty. May she be well taught in heavenly lore. May she be fruitful in offspring. May her life be good and sinless. May she win the rest of the blessed and the kingdom of heaven. May they both see their children's children unto the third and fourth generation, and may they reach the old age they desire. Amen.

Heavenly Father, let the faith of Your children never falter, but increase our hope in Your promises to us. Amen.

Sadie, Sally, Sarah

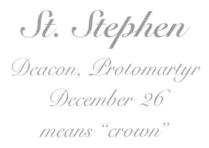

St. Stephen
Deacon, Protomartyr
December 26
means "crown"

Stephen was chosen by the faithful to be one of the "seven men of good character full of the Holy Ghost and wisdom" who were ordained the first deacons by the Apostles. The Acts of the Apostles also records that "Stephen, full of grace and fortitude, did great wonders and signs among the people." Some Jewish elders plotted to kill Stephen and succeeded in doing so by stoning him to death on the false charge of blasphemy. As he was dying, he pleaded, "Lord, lay not this sin to their charge." Saul, whom we now know as St. Paul, held the discarded cloaks of those who stoned Stephen. St. Stephen is the patron of stone workers, bricklayers, and casket makers because his coffin was found and his relics were translated on December 26, while 73 persons who witnessed this were healed.

St. Stephen of Hungary ◆ September 22

On September 2, Geysa, the Duke of Hungary saw St. Stephen the protomartyr in a vision who told him that he would have a son who would perfect the work he had begun. Geysa and his wife, both converts, had a son in A.D. 977 and named him Stephen. He succeeded his father at an early age, rooted out idolatry, suppressed pagan rebellion and founded churches and monasteries. He became king and placed Hungary under the protection of Our Lady. His was a wise and holy sovereignty. Although all of his children preceded him in death, he accepted the Will of God and remained steadfast in his love for God. After disposing his kingdom into proper hands for its prosperous future, he died in peace on his favorite feast of Mary's Assumption in 1038. The feast day of St. Stephen of Hungary is September 22.

St. Stephen, may I have courage like yours so that I will be willing to pay any price to testify to my faith in Jesus. Amen.

Steven, Stefan, Stevie, Stephanie, Stephana, Esteban, Estevan

St. Susanna

Old Testament Heroine

August 11

means "lily"

In the twelfth chapter of the book of the prophet Daniel, the story of Susanna is recounted. Susanna was a beautiful, God-fearing woman. She was married to Joakim, a Jew in Babylon who was wealthy and the most respected of all the Jews. Two Jewish elders who were appointed judges over the people that year frequented Joakim's house to consult him on matters. They were sinfully attracted to Susanna, and knew she would walk through her husband's garden and bathe there on occasion. One day, they surprised her there alone and threatened her to give in to their desires, or they would accuse her of being with a young man. Susanna, not wanting to offend her God, screamed and the two elders ran out. The next day Susanna was brought before all the people to be tried and condemned to death. She prayed to God for deliverance, while the elders testified falsely against her. Just as she was about to be put to death, the prophet Daniel, who was only a small child in the crowd, spoke up and rebuked his people for their unjust trial. Daniel cross-examined the two elders and discovered their treachery upon which they received the death sentence Susanna was about to receive. "Thus was innocent blood spared that day" thanks to the worthy supplications of Susanna and the wisdom of Daniel.

St. Susanna, a noble Roman martyr, was the niece of Pope Caius who had made a vow of virginity refusing to marry, on which account she was cruelly but with heroic constancy martyred by Diocletian in about 295. Her body lies in stational church of St. Susanna in Rome with those of St. Felicity and St. Genesius. Her feast day is August 11.

O God, may those who are imprisoned, accused guilty, yet innocent, call upon You who only desire the freedom, happiness, and salvation of all of Your beloved children. Amen.

Susan, Sukey, Suzanne, Sue, Lilly

St. Teresa of Avila

Doctor of the Church
October 15
means "carrying ears of corn"

Born at Avila, Spain in 1515, Teresa was a very precocious child. When she turned twenty, Teresa joined the Carmelite convent. Over time, she too was caught up in the mediocrity and worldliness that seeped into the convent. Stirred by God's grace, Teresa began to reform the abuses found in the Carmelite convents. She founded a new Carmelite house in Avila that returned to the original rule. The nuns of this reform were called "discalced" (without shoes) Carmelites. By the time of her death in 1582, Teresa had founded seventeen discalced convents throughout Spain. She was declared a Doctor of the Church in 1970 for the spiritual wisdom she passed on to the Church. In this picture she is teaching her nuns about the interior castle, symbolizing the seven dwelling places of the soul in its journey to God, Who is in the center of the castle. She is the patron of aviators and the elderly. She is also invoked by those who suffer from headaches because she had so many, and heart attacks because she received a severe wound of love in her heart for God by a small seraph that pierced her heart with a flaming arrow. Doctors confirmed that her heart remained incorrupt.

Quote of St. Teresa:
"Let nothing disturb you, let nothing frighten you, though all things pass, God does not change. Patience wins all things, but he lacks nothing who possesses God, for God alone suffices."

Holy Spirit, inspire us to reform our own lives and correct our bad habits so that like St. Teresa, we may be examples of conversion and self-denial for the sake of Your Kingdom and the salvation of many souls. Amen.

Tracy, Terry, Tessa, Therese, Teresia

St. Thomas

Apostle and Martyr

July 3

means "twin"

Jesus chose Thomas, a simple tent maker in Galilee as one of the twelve. Thomas is often dubbed "the doubter" based on his lack of faith in the disciples' words when they said they had seen the resurrected Christ. Thomas scoffed, and said he would not believe unless he had tangible proof, unless he himself could touch Jesus' wounds. Jesus appeared again, and it seemed He did so for Thomas alone so that Thomas could probe Jesus' wounds. Thomas then exclaimed, "My Lord, and my God!" (John 20:24-29). Thomas' sanctity, in spite of his apparent lack of faith, serves both as encouragement and admonishment for the faithful who seek tangible proof in order to believe God. However, he should be equally remembered for his personal love for his Master when he showed his willingness to die with his Savior (John 14:5), and when he expresses his fear of being separated from Jesus (John 11:16).

After Pentecost, Thomas went to evangelize in Asia, probably in Persia and as far as India, and the Apostle, who finally believed because he had probed Jesus' spear wound, suffered martyrdom by spearing in Mylapore. The first spearing brought Thomas' fingers into Jesus' wound; the second spearing drew him into the Heart of God forever.

Thomas is the patron of those who doubt.

"You shall make them princes through all the land; they shall remember Your name, O Lord". Gradual from the Mass of Holy Apostle
  ~ Psalm 44:17

"You who have followed Me shall sit on thrones judging the twelve tribes of Israel."
  Communion ~ Matt 19, 28

My Lord, and my God, let me not falter in my faith, but rather be a faith-filled apostle in a world that seeks evidence to believe in You. Amen.

Tom, Tommy, Tomas, Thomasina, Tammy, Tamzine

~ 159 ~

St. Thomas Aquinas

Doctor of the Church
January 28
means "twin"

Born to a noble family in 1226, Thomas was expected to become a knight or soldier, but instead he wished to be a Dominican friar. His decision was not met without resistance from his family. Being a brilliant student, Thomas' superiors sent him to Cologne, Germany to study under St. Albert the Great. On the way there however, his brothers kidnapped him and locked him in the family tower for two years in an effort to dissuade him, employing immoral tactics to break his resolve to follow the religious life. Finally, his sisters helped him to escape. Thomas continued his journey and went on to become one of the best minds in all of history. His theological work, particularly the Summa Theologia, is still the basis of modern theology. He died at the age of forty-seven in 1274. Thomas had a special devotion to the Eucharist and today we sing his Latin hymns such as "Pange Lingua" and "Tantum Ergo." He is the patron saint of Catholic schools, theologians, pencil makers, and clear weather. He is called "The Angelic Doctor" because of his purity and wisdom.

Quotes of St. Thomas Aquinas:
"As sailors are guided by a star to the port, so are Christians guided to Heaven by Mary."
"To love God is something greater than to know him."
"Charity is the form, mover, mother, and root of all the virtues."
"To know whom to avoid is a great means of saving our souls."
"Take care not to give way to drunkenness because this sin so disgraces mankind, that it lowers them beneath the unreasoning animal."

Father of wisdom, You inspired St. Thomas Aquinas to study sacred truths so as to know and love You better. May we learn to know and love You through St. Thomas' teaching and intercession. Amen.

Tom, Tommy, Tomas, Thomasina, Tammy, Tamzine

St. Thomas More

Martyr

June 22

means "twin"

Thomas was born in Chelsea, England in 1478. He studied law and entered Parliament in 1504. After discerning that his vocation was not to become a priest, he married in 1505 and had four children. His wife Jane died prematurely and, for the sake of their children, he remarried. Thomas was very intelligent, humorous, and witty. He exuded joy and love for life, yet lived with a deep spirit of self-sacrifice. Henry VIII ascended to the throne of England and appointed Thomas, whose company he enjoyed, his chancellor in 1529. The king's shallow admiration for Thomas turned to hatred when Thomas refused to approve of the king's disobedience and defiance towards the Catholic Church. Thomas was imprisoned in the Tower of London and beheaded on July 6, 1535 for defending the truth of Christ's Church. He is the patron saint of lawyers, politicians, statesmen, widowers, and stepparents.

Another Englishman, St. Thomas a'Becket, was Bishop of Canterbury. When King Henry II was doing harm to the Church, Thomas courageously opposed the king at the risk of his own life. He died at the hands of Nobles in a church in front of the altar. His feast day is December 29.

Quote of St. Thomas More:
"What does it avail to know that there is a God which thou not only believest by faith, but also knowest by reason. What does it avail that thou knowest Him if thou think little of Him."

Dear Jesus, St. Thomas imitated Your death in his martyrdom for witnessing to the truth. Let us never deny the truth we find in our consciences and therefore be witnesses to Your Divine Law in our hearts. Amen.

Tom, Tomas, Thomasina, Tamzine, Tammy, Chelsea

St. Timothy

Bishop and Martyr
January 26
means "fearing God"

Timothy was of Greek and Jewish lineage. His mother was Eunice, and his grandmother was Lois. St. Paul wrote two Epistles to his disciple, St. Timothy. In the second epistle of St. Paul to Timothy Chapter 1:5 we read, "calling to mind that faith which is in thee unfeigned, which also dwelt first in thy grandmother Lois, and in thy mother Eunice, and I am certain that in thee also." Timothy is thought to have had a diffident and nervous temperament, yet he was enthusiastic enough to need a warning from St. Paul to look after his health. For this reason, Timothy is the patron of stomach ailments. Beloved of Paul, Timothy was asked by Paul to come and comfort him in his last hours. Timothy was the first Bishop of Ephesus where St. John the Evangelist died and Our Lady visited and lived there in the latter part of her life. There also the Third Ecumenical Council of the Church took place. The Council of Ephesus, as it was called, defended the Divine Maternity of Mary. St. Timothy was stoned to death for defending Mary's virginity and for attacking the Greek goddess, Diana of the Ephesians. There is good evidence that his relics had been enshrined in Constantinople and supernatural manifestations took place there as related both by St. Chrysostom and St. Jerome.

O God, through St. Paul You entrusted to Bishop Timothy the government of several churches. Grant that we may lovingly pray for our shepherds who have this great responsibility and so remain united in filial obedience to the Holy See. Amen.

Tim, Eunice, Lois

O MARY, CONCEIVED WITHOUT SIN PRAY FOR US WHO HAVE RECOURSE TO YOU.

The Virgin of the Globe

The first apparition of Our Lady to St. Catherine Laboure is that of Our Lady of the Globe. The golden globe symbolized all the global prayers offered to God through Mary. In this apparition, Mary wore gem-studded rings on her fingers from which rays of graces streamed down upon the earth, making it rich and fruitful. As Catherine watched, Mary's arms swung down to her side, as depicted in the first Miraculous Medal that is also known as the second apparition.

On September 10, 1991 St. Catherine Laboure spoke internally to Mary Kathryn Johnson for the first time. It was time for the Virgin of the Globe medal to be produced and distributed. The first medals were introduced to the public on September 17, 1994. The medal is meant to promulgate the fifth and final Marian dogma: Mary, Co-redemptrix, Mediatrix, and Advocate for the people of God.

Blessed Mother Teresa of Calcutta held the Miraculous Medal in highest regard. She knew of the miraculous intercessory power of the Blessed Mother's prayer. It was Teresa's custom to kiss blessed Miraculous Medals and to distribute them.

Novena to the Virgin of the Globe

O Mary, conceived without sin, CO-REDEMPTRIX-willing Participant in Jesus' great work of salvation, teach us to work with Him for the salvation of our neighbor. Pray for us who have recourse to Thee!

O Mary, conceived without sin, MEDIATRIX of all graces and Mother of every soul, let the graces we receive through your hands be met with profound gratitude and sincere cooperation. Pray for us who have recourse to Thee!

O Mary, conceived without sin, ADVOCATE for the people of God, from the moment of the Annunciation until the end of time, lift up our deeply wounded world to God's merciful love. Pray for us who have recourse to thee!

Virginia, Ginny

St. William of Bourges

Belonging to an illustrious family in Nevers, France, William DonJeon was made a canon first in Soissons then in Paris. Soon after, he felt the call to become a Cistercian monk. So sweet, humble, and austere a soul could not remain hidden, and he was chosen abbot. However, the archbishop of Bourges died and three Cistercian abbots were voted upon to be his successor. William was chosen, but since all three were worthy and fit, they prayed and drew cards; his name was on all three. He redoubled his fast, abstinence, and penance. As an archbishop he was gentle but inflexible against abuses and confiscation, even from the king. He was very busy converting many Albigensian heretics, but a high fever overtook him and he died on January 10, 1209. His body, honored by many miracles, was interred in his cathedral.

William of York was the son of Earl Herbert and Emma, King St. Stephen of Hungary's sister. Dedicated to his faith, he followed the calling to be ordained a priest. In 1144 he was elected as Archbishop of York and rejected when he asked Rome to accept the other candidate whom certain monks wanted instead. He happily returned to seclusion until that bishop died. As he was again elected and tried to enter his diocese, two men forbade him but the entire bridge collapsed into the river before him including many of the faithful coming to welcome him. The saintly man raised his eyes in prayer to God, and the whole multitude escaped unharmed. Even when William suffered rejection, slander and calumny, his humility and meekness never allowed him to seek revenge or harbor resentment. His feast day is June 8.

Meekness and humility are rare qualities in any human, but especially in a great leader. O God, because of Your grace, William was such. Through his prayers, may we become meek and humble like little children and "raise as a delightful fragrance about Your throne". Amen.

Will, Willy, Bill, Billy, Wilma, Wilhemina

St. Zachary

Father of John the Baptist
November 5
means "remembered of Jehovah"

While the aged Jewish priest was performing his duties in the Temple of Jerusalem, an angel appeared to him saying, "Zachary, do not be afraid; your prayer has been heard, and your wife Elizabeth is to bear a son to whom you shall give the name of John." The angel told Zachary that his son would be filled with the Holy Spirit in his mother's womb and would bring many Israelites back to God, thus preparing the way for the Messiah.

Because Zachary doubted this wonderful news of salvation, he was struck dumb until the day his baby son was to be named. In his house the Virgin Mary stayed and helped Elizabeth until the birth. Later at the circumcision, Zachary wrote on his wax tablet, "His name is John." In great joy Zachary then spoke for the first time in nine months the beautiful canticle of praise, the "Benedictus." It is now part of the daily Liturgy of the Hours.

Zachary is believed to been martyred because he would not reveal the whereabouts of his son whom Herod sought to kill.

Benedictus

Blessed be the Lord, the God of Israel; he has come to his people and set them free. He has raised up for us a mighty savior, born of the house of his servant David.
Through his holy prophets he promised of old that he would save us from our enemies, from the hands of all who hate us.
He promised to show mercy to our fathers and to remember his holy covenant.
This was the oath he swore to our father Abraham: to set us free from the hands of our enemies, free to worship him without fear, holy and righteous in his sight all the days of our life.

You, my child, shall be called the prophet of the Most High, for you will go before the Lord to prepare his way, to give his people knowledge of salvation by the forgiveness of their sins.
In the tender compassion of our God the dawn from on high shall break upon us, to shine on those who dwell in darkness and the shadow of death, and to guide our feet into the way of peace.

Zack, Zachariah

Holy Cards/Prints

Laminated Holy Cards (may be mixed)

Single copies	$.75 each	plus S&H
10-24	$.70 each	plus S&H
25 or more	$.65 each	plus S&H

Quality Watercolor Prints
Call for sizes and pricing

Ammccallum, Inc.
10930 243rd Street
Scandia, MN 55073
(320) 396-3764
(651) 257-6324

www.ammccallum.com
ammccallum@usfamily.net

This book, holy cards or prints will be a delightful gift
for your family and friends - birthdays, anniversaries, Christmas, Easter